Decades of
DISCOVERY
Free to be me

Decades of DISCOVERY

Free to be me

*To Maggie
with love from
Margaret.*

MARGARET MAUND

y Lolfa

In memory of our beloved parents,
Doris and Donald Maund

First impression: 2011

© Copyright Margaret Maund and Y Lolfa Cyf., 2011

Cover design: Y Lolfa
Cover photograph: Clive Davies

ISBN: 978 184771 262 2

FSC
Published and printed in Wales
on paper from well maintained forests
by Y Lolfa Cyf., Talybont, Ceredigion SY24 5HE
website www.ylolfa.com
e-mail ylolfa@ylolfa.com
tel 01970 832 304
fax 832 782

Contents

FOREWORD

SOME PEOPLE ARE born storytellers. The Reverend Margaret Maund is one such person as can be seen from this, her autobiography. Over the years she has regaled her fellow students, fellow nurses, missionaries, radio listeners and parishioners with tales of her colourful life.

The first period spans the early years in Tonyrefail, nursing training in the Rhondda, studying midwifery in Cardiff, a year in Belgium learning French, and several years nursing in Pimu in the Belgian Congo with the Baptist Missionary Society. After returning to Wales, just before her father's death, and discovering that returning to the Congo was no longer an option, because of the deterioration in her health, other adventures followed. Margaret became a midwife tutor, a Sister in a residential home, and Anglican non-stipendiary priest, a hospital chaplain and a Cruse counsellor in Cardiff Prison. Needless to say many amusing incidents occurred in the course of these varied activities. These are shared with the reader. Margaret has a great sense of humour and a very infectious laugh, and is able to laugh about her own misfortunes. She does however gloss over her difficulties. Despite making it very clear that her Christian faith is the anchor of her life, she has known the 'dark night of the soul' following her parents' death, and other family tragedies, and is very honest about her struggles. We can therefore identify more fully with her.

In the last chapter Margaret sums up her adventures with a revealing quote from a local newspaper: 'The aim of life is not to edge towards the grave slowly to be placed silently inside, rather to hurtle towards it and skid in sideways yelling, "Wow, that was a heck of a ride."'

We have enjoyed sharing Margaret's story so far, and

since she is still writing, we hope that we shall be able to continue to skid along with her in the future!

Rev. Saunders Davies
May 2011

INTRODUCTION

'LAUGH AND THE world laughs with you,' goes the old saying, but the chances of that happening today it seems are becoming increasingly rarer. It is said that we are laughing much less than we did fifty years ago. Modern-day life seems to have created a stressed out society, where worries, a falling standard of living and paying the bills override everything else.

Now and again we all experience the depressing effects of the doom and gloom merchants. They look miserable, rejoice in bad news and wallow in other peoples problems. Looking on the more positive and brighter side doesn't seem possible for them.

Laughter it seems improves our health. Our forefathers knew this when archaeological digs found healing temples next to theatres. Patients would hear the laughter and get better quicker. There is a beauty bonus as well it seems. Laughter and smiles lift and soften the face resulting in a broad smile which can be seen by another human being up to a hundred and fifty yards away.

Sadly it seems we may be afraid to be happy. Children smile, we are told, four hundred times a day; an adult only managing fifteen smiles a day. Children laugh one hundred and fifty times a day; an adult six times in one day.

Can anyone imagine Jesus straight faced and miserable in the middle of an Eastern wedding where he would be surrounded by exuberance, joy and laughter? I often think of these words about God. 'He will fill your mouth with laughter and shouts of joy will be on your lips' and 'God has given me reason to laugh and everybody who hears will laugh with me.'

Friends and colleagues in work and church often say to me "tell us a story", thoroughly enjoying the many situations which have made up my life. Most stories are a constant source of fun, and right across the age range we have laughed together. Perhaps there is something in what the researchers say about the power of laughter to keep us healthy.

I trust you will enjoy these stories from my life. Perhaps you'll take the advice of one of my friends, "I'm not taking your stories into hospital – I'll burst my stitches." Laugh and smile, share the joy and sadness and marvel at the rich fabric of life which makes us who we are.

Margaret Maund
May 2011

ACKNOWLEDGEMENTS

I would like to thank the following:

My brother David, for his consistent support.

Salem Chapel, for nurturing me from childhood to adult years.

The Baptist Missionary Society, for preparing me and sending me to Africa, where I had some of the most unforgettable years of my life.

The Bishop Saunders Davies and Cynthia, for their love and support over many years, especially during the writing of my autobiography.

The Church in Wales and all those, too many to mention, in the non-stipendiary ministry: friends, colleagues, tutors and priests for launching me into a new phase and fulfilling and completing my first love.

The Reverends Vivian Parkinson and Ian Hodges, for sharing my retirement, and taking no notice of it whatsoever!

Julie Morgan, for helping me over the past year.

Sheryll, Bethan and Rhidian, for typing the early scripts.

My friends at Vogue Salon, Tonyrefail, for keeping my hair in order!

Nurses and midwifery friends, for many long years of friendship and fun.

My family and friends everywhere, for sharing my life, bringing much joy and happiness over the years and into the future.

Thank you all
Margaret

1

In the Beginning

I RUSHED INTO the world during a blackout, arriving at the same time as a baby boy. Mother told me years later that there was confusion right from the start. I didn't look like anybody in the family for years and the question often popped up, "What time was the other baby born? A boy wasn't it?"

Father celebrated in the usual way in the colliery where he worked, and arrived for visiting hour a little merry, hotfooting it to the cot to see his new baby son. He wasn't exactly pleased when I gazed back at him, all 6½ lbs of squealing female flesh, and he almost did what they told him to do at the colliery, "send her back", at least that's the version I got. I suspect it was a more colourful response.

Somewhere in Bridgend there might have been another mother gazing at her son looking for a familiar family feature, who knows? Occasionally one of my relatives would say, "Well, she is beginning to look like cousin so and so and auntie somebody else." It didn't matter anyway, my father was soon reconciled to me and his son turned up two years and two months later.

Our mother wasn't born in London and always called herself a cockney and most certainly had the accent to prove it. Dad turned up at the family house in 691 Fulham Road, having been sent to the city to learn a trade during the depression in Wales.

There were three girls in the family, but the story goes that Dad took one look at Mum, and decided that nobody else would do. After completing his training, Dad returned to Wales telling Mum that he would be back in three weeks for an answer to his marriage proposal. Mum packed her bags and settled in Coedely to make plans for her wedding.

As we were growing up, making frequent trips to our large family in London was wonderful for us. We often posed the question, "How did you settle down in a place so very different from your home?" Mum just smiled and Dad would laugh when she said, "I followed your father."

Dad and his family were Anglicans (Church in Wales) which was the place to be in our growing up days. Subsequently, my brother David and I were both christened a few weeks after birth.

Mum however was an English Baptist and had belonged to a local fellowship near her home in London since she was a teenager.

The local chapel, Salem English Baptist, was not far away from the housing estate where we lived – only one road to cross, with Sunday school teachers waiting to see us safely over. The church, however, was three roads away with a large field to walk across. So, my brother David and I joined the Baptist Sunday school when we were primary school age although my father's family didn't altogether approve.

My first memories were of going into the vestry behind the chapel with lots of other small children. We stayed there until we were seven years of age. There were huge pictures on the wall showing Moses receiving the Ten Commandments, and of the narrow road leading to heaven and the wide road leading to destruction. One large poster attracted me straight away and I loved the stories our teachers told us about the people in the pictures. Jesus is walking along the beach with six children, all holding hands. Jesus held the hand of a little boy who was different from any child I had ever seen before. The teachers explained that the children lived in other countries, where the sun was very hot and the children had dark skin to stop them from burning and they wore different clothes. This picture left a huge impression on me because, tucked into the side of the frame, was a little girl in a gymslip and she looked just like me. I was too young to read the words underneath, but another Sunday school teacher told us that Jesus loved all the children in the world and said to all of them, 'Follow Me'.

We were soon to experience the joys of Sunday school parties with lots of jelly, cakes and custard. I think Dave and I enjoyed our first orange in Sunday school, most certainly tasting our first grapes with sticky juice rolling down our chins and fingers. Sunday school trips were the highlight of the year. Six double-decker buses parked outside the chapel on the hill, and soon filled with hundreds of very excited children, parents, and anybody else who could fit in. Armed with buckets and spades, pocket money, sandwiches and Corona pop, we set off for the sands of Barry one year and Porthcawl, the next.

I remember one trip in particular when David was about eight years old. We were given 2/6d. to spend, which is about 12 pence in today's money. It was supposed to last us all day but David had different ideas. Sitting in the front of the bus with Dad, they were the ones first off. Dave went straight to the kiosk in front of him and spent his whole day's allowance on a long black telescope before Mum and I had put a foot on the ground. We teased him over the years, pointing out the same kiosk when we were both adults telling the same tale to his son and his grandchildren. They always asked, "But Dad (or Granddad), didn't you have any sweets or ice-cream or fair rides at all?"

The fair was the highlight of the trip with all of us going en masse an hour before the buses were due to leave at 6 p.m. We screamed our way through the ghost train, swapping that, some years later, for the tunnel of love when the first boyfriends came on the scene. We were soaked on the water chute, knocked about on the dodgems and sticky with candyfloss and toffee apples. David never missed out on anything, even though his money was gone before the day had started.

They were all wonderful happy times. Nothing could replace the joy of the trip to the seaside, both places now only twenty minutes away in a car. I still recall the unforgettable sound of children's voices. "I can see the sea! Look it's over there! I can see the sea!"

2

Childhood

WE MOVED OUT of the primary class when we were seven, and went into the middle vestry where we were soon enthralled with stories about Mary Jones and her Bible. From then on, we moved around the classes in the big chapel, until we arrived in 'the big class' at the age of fourteen. Bible class took over after that but, with one thing and another, I never got there.

I would have loved to have moved up to the Bible class but was too young. "Sixteen, Margaret," said the pastor. "You can come then." Enviously I watched a large group, including my beloved Dad, all photographed looking very smart in dark blazers and grey trousers with the ladies in pretty frocks. I never did join that Bible class, as life began to open up with some of its amazing twists and turns.

Fifty years later, with most of the original class now in their early sixties, we were reunited to celebrate the 200th anniversary of our little chapel. This time I was in the photograph alongside everybody else who had been there fifty years before.

Our lives had followed many different paths in the intervening years. Trevor and Eirwen Jones, chapel friends, had married when we were young and they stayed in Salem all their lives. Trevor became the pastor just a few years ago, something which none of us would have dreamt of when we were all Salem chapel youth.

As a child, I soaked it all up like a sponge and right from

the beginning often got more than my share. Mum was asked to join the sisterhood but regretfully said no. I was the reason apparently as, still primary school age, I didn't like my mother out of the house, although Dad was home to look after us both.

"Bring her with you," said the pastor. I joined about fifty other women in the vestry, wonderfully heated by a coal burning stove. One special memory from then was cutting the birthday cake with the pastor's mother, who was eighty when I was eight years old. I attended for years and Mum never missed a meeting.

Added to this were Junior Endeavour, Intermediates and Senior Christian Endeavour groups, and Mum and Dad both became presidents of these. I was playing the piano by now, aged seven, having being taught by the pastor, the Rev. W J Uppington. David followed along as well with both of us learning enough to play reasonably well many years later. We had an active music group in Salem with violins, flutes and a piano. I don't think we had guitars with us then, although good singing made up for that. They were very happy days and I embraced my chapel life with all the enthusiasm I could muster, enjoying all the activities that filled up most of the week.

Some family members, including my paternal grandmother, felt that we were missing out and should be given more opportunities. Well, there was the local fleapit, with old films on show, mostly westerns, which David loved and still does to this day. There was a roller skating rink at the end of the park, and a swimming pool a bus ride away. There were Brownies and Guides, Cubs and Scouts. There were plenty of boys in chapel and I was always in the middle of a crowd. I didn't feel there was anything missing; in fact there was more going on than I could handle.

Chapel anniversaries were the highlight of the year. People came from miles around: a well-known fact being that if you were not in a seat by 5.30 p.m. for 6 p.m. then you just wouldn't get in. Extra chairs and standing room still left crowds milling around the vestries and lawn outside. In spite of my early immersion into chapel life, I never participated fully until I was much older. One year, I joined Gaynor, both of us in new dresses, and stood up when cued by the pastor. One head to the left, the other to the right, family waiting with bated breath, we did just manage to say loudly together, "God is love."

As Salem was an English Baptist chapel, people were baptized by total immersion. I witnessed many and lustily joined in the hymn singing after each one.

Follow, Follow I Will Follow Jesus
Anywhere, Everywhere I Will Follow Him.

Mum had given me a children's Bible a number of years before with lots of shiny coloured pictures in it. One image in particular stayed with me: Jesus on the cross at Calvary. I clearly knew then that Jesus had died for me. It was powerful and personal: 'I did it for you.'

Around about the same time, a number of teenagers and adults were being prepared for baptism and on the Tuesday evening before the Sunday, I startled my parents by saying that I would like to be baptised. Dad walked a few streets to see the pastor (no phones then), whose response was that if Margaret wanted to be baptised, he would baptise me.

I joined the rest on a bitterly cold winter's night wearing a long white dress with elastic around the bottom (so that the skirt would not come over my head, I was told), and waist length brown plaits. I was only ten years old. "Stay on the bottom step," said the pastor, "you will drown if you stand in the tank." I came out of the water to the usual singing of 'Follow, Follow I Will Follow Jesus'. All I knew really was that I loved this kind gentle man with all the children of the world around Him and that I had now joined them as well. I had no understanding of some of those sombre lines in the hymn.

> Where the storms are sweeping
> And the dark waters flow.

I didn't know anything about danger or the 'fear of the valley or upon the mountain steep'. It would take the rest of my life to appreciate the true meaning of those familiar words which I had sung with such enthusiasm in my teenage years.

3

School Days

SCHOOL DAYS PROVED unremarkable. I wasn't doing too badly on the whole and it was anticipated that I might just gain the all-important 11+. I can see Mum's face now, all these years later, crumple with the disappointment. There wasn't much else for the rest of us really; there was such a sad division between secondary modern and grammar school education then. Mum and Dad said very little, as they did when David failed a couple of years later. They said to both of us, "You have done your best. We shall go and buy the blue and gold uniform for Gellidawel," where we were both destined to spend the next four years.

There was a lot of unkindness felt between 'us' Gellidawel and 'them' the grammar school, now that we were relegated to the bottom of the pile. Jeering at navy blue uniforms instead of green; crossing the street with no words exchanged from one to the other. I don't think Dave or I felt the sense of failure. Mum and Dad were too positive to let that happen. After all, eleven years old is a bit young to think about a job and the need for O and A levels. We settled down, Dave and I, in 'sec mod', but my mother's expression stayed with me for years. The unkindness was a sharp shock to someone who had been nurtured in chapel, sheltered from unpleasantness and cruel remarks. The big wide world was getting closer and it was not as cosy and warm as it had been. I suppose it all went deep into my subconscious as I never wear green to this very day and I cultivated a healthy dislike for the grammar school and all it stood for, for years to come.

David was different. He had a hearty dislike for chapel and anything that went on in there. His apathy, boredom and loud sighing so embarrassed my parents that they saw no point in him being there. Some time later a friendly neighbour arrived with a small black and white television set. Dave settled in at home and, for the first time on a Sunday, enjoyed himself.

Mum became a very popular speaker visiting sisterhoods and various meetings all over the place. One evening Mum realized that she was speaking too far away to return home by bus. "Don't worry Mum," said Dave, "I'll come and fetch you." Dave was working by now and driving his first car. While he was waiting for Mum a young man put his head through the open car window. "Why not come to the youth club, Dave? It's on every Wednesday 6–8 p.m." The following week Dave showered and shaved, "Where are you going Dave?" asked our parents. "I thought I'd take a look at the youth club," he replied. David never left Pont-y-clun Baptist church after that, and he was baptised by full immersion when he was nineteen years of age, ten years after leaving our little chapel on the hill.

His life from that time on turned right around and would hold a few surprises, as mine would, in time to come.

4

Growing Up

AT FOURTEEN YEARS of age we all visited a careers officer and at the time I was only interested in anything with four legs: horses first, dogs second, which wasn't a lot of help really. Tiny children came in third and nursery work had some attraction. Mother got a bit fed up and took matters into her own hands. She went off to see the manager of the local Co-op chemist (clutching her black book to her chest). I could start when I was fifteen and Mum was very pleased.

The whole prospect filled me with horror. Well, mental arithmetic was never a strong point and there were no helpful tills as there are today. The prospect of an ever-growing queue while I tried to work out the change filled me with dismay. My headmaster, Mr Phillips, came up with a brilliant solution. "You're fond of children," he said, "What about training to be a nurse? Then you can specialise afterwards." Anything was better than the chemist, so I said I'd have a try.

About six of us sat the examination, joining the rest of the Rhondda applicants. School days, as I said, were unremarkable but these exams taken at almost fifteen years old were remarkable – I passed! What a turn up for the books! My parents' delight knew no bounds. I gained a place in another school for a year and began what seemed a very long journey to become a nurse.

Off came the long plaits – in came a frizzy perm. I should never have let that happen; my hair has never recovered since. Out went the gold and navy uniform and in came pale blue and navy. Out went a few minutes walk to school – in came a fairly long bus journey.

It was a good year though, learning maths, biology, physics and science. We bathed and dressed china dolls, took temperatures and pulses, bandaged limbs and learned how to make a bed. We visited clinics and doctors' surgeries and the local hospital, and for a change I was now getting on reasonably well. Soon, we were sixteen and a half years of age, old enough to visit matron, leave school, get a job and earn some money. Life was certainly beginning to look up.

I didn't realise until years later what huge sacrifices my parents made to buy yet another uniform, a complete school kit and keep me in school for an extra year. Without that love and commitment right at the very beginning, none of the rest of my life, as it unfolded, could have happened.

A couple of weeks later, six of us were seen nervously standing outside matron's door. After being subjected to interviews, medicals, X-rays and blood tests, we were relieved to hear her say, "I'll have you all." We had become pre-nursing students shortened to PNS.

I was reminded frequently over the years that I faced my future employer with a specific piece of underwear under my arm; there just wasn't time to put it back on. Nevertheless my rather untidy start was to mark the beginning of a very busy and challenging new life.

We spent a lot of time in casualty, in the corridor outside the operating theatres, blood banks, diet kitchen and occasionally maternity. A familiar cry followed us everywhere. Our names were ignored – PNS sounded along every corridor – Pee, Nnn, Ess was heard so many times in an average day, so many tasks, so many errands, so many jokes, why haven't you brought elbow grease from the pharmacy and, what took you so long? Tidy that cupboard! Fold those

23

sheets! Clean the inkwells and yes you can go in the plaster room as long as you wash the floor afterwards!

We wore white starched dresses and very complicated hats that sat on the top of our heads and fell into frills at the back. Mother proudly took a photograph. Looking at that now, I cannot believe that anybody would let us near them.

One particular time I was based in a large outpatients department. I first had to collect the patients' notes from the reception desk, make a list for the doctors' rooms and then call out their names as they waited their turn in very busy clinics.

Unknown to me, a neighbour was passing through the department and went straight home to tell Mum that I had been seen working in the hospital. Also unknown to me until years later, I found out that Mum had taken the next bus, bought herself a sandwich and a cup of tea from the WRVS and, at a safe distance, watched me working for the rest of the day. At last she could relax. I was fine and earning a little, perhaps only a couple of pounds a week, if I remember correctly.

By this time David was working in the local bakery. Mum took the same delight in watching him bake bread and cakes and stack them into waiting delivery vans. Mum and Dad were well over their early disappointment. We were both doing all right after all.

As for us pre-nurses, we longed for the day when we turned eighteen and would have a proper dress and cap and be ready for 'block'. That very special day did come – twelve weeks in 'block', a set of examinations and, at last, a decent uniform: navy blue pinstriped dress, starched white apron, blue elastic belt and frilly cuffs around short sleeves. A small white hat on top of the head, black stockings and black lace up shoes set it all off. When I gazed at that lot for the first time, I couldn't believe my eyes; a proper nursing uniform and the very early beginnings of a proper nurse.

The six of us stuck together having roamed around the hospital for the best part of two years. We knew the place inside out. Life in the hospital was hard work with shifts and a 42-hour working week. However, our new lives were exciting and full of fun most of the time. Night duty was especially chatty, often passing the long night away with a baby on each arm, when sent to the busy children's ward. We faced endless milk feeds, nappy changing, potty training and medicine being spat back in our faces. Needless to say, we loved it all.

5

Student Nurses

"You'll be my bridesmaid Maud," said my friend Padfield in the early hours of one morning (we were both on nights). We never used Christian names, the 'n' having been dropped from my surname Maund much earlier.

"No, certainly not," said matron when we both, of course, requested the same time off. Pleas of "But I'm the bride matron," followed by "And I'm the bridesmaid," failed to change her mind. "That doesn't make the slightest scrap of difference," was the only response that we had.

Much wheedling and cajoling of friends to change a shift saw me following Padfield (her Christian name was Janet) down the aisle a few weeks later. But as I had replaced my shift, I had to prove that I had been there. "I want a photograph," matron (who was never one to give up easily) said, and I proudly showed that to her when I was sent for. I can see her face now, gazing at me photographed in a stiff blue dress, underskirts bristling with net and two blue roses fastened drunkenly on the top of my head. "It was a lovely day, it really was matron." "Very well nurse but don't let it happen again," marked the end of that.

I never did any harm and the whole lot of us never caused any damage but we were high spirited and mischievous, spending a fair bit of our training outside matron's door. "Come on in out of the rain nurse," ordered the Sister, sharply rapping her fingernails against the window. "Will you listen to me nurse, at once, I said, at once?" Sister called in vain. Just around the corner we lurked in the darkness, fists stuffed into our mouths, shaking with glee. Millie, the school dummy had done it again. Millie was made of a soft, grey fabric and was unclothed, bald and glassy-eyed. Generations of students were taught how to dress her, change her position on the hospital bed and practise making the bed with Millie in it, before being let loose on real live patients. She often appeared, sitting at the bus stop, never getting on the bus that frequently turned up. "You'd better fetch Millie back, the juniors have been at it again," was a frequent order from the lodge. She was also responsible for a blood-curdling yell shattering the night air when an unsuspecting trainee found her in bed. (We were very fond of Millie but she was very old and not a very pretty sight.) Millie was locked up in the end, but not before we had our funs worth first.

I can well remember another time when matron said that she'd never heard anything like it in her life. I had come off duty about 9 p.m. absolutely shattered and tumbled into a hot bath and was soon fast asleep in my little single bed. It was very dark when I woke up and I knew that something was different. I found *my* two feet, then a third. My screams filled the early morning air. "Murder nurse, murder. That's what I thought," said Home Sister. "Well, really Maud," said McNamara (one of the six – we never called her Ann either). "I didn't get back until 11 p.m. and my door was locked, yours was open, so I got in with you!" I was in trouble again, for screaming that time, not for being two in a bed.

The day dawned when new experiences at another hospital came about at the end of our first year. It was right by the sea, wonderful; three months of specialist nursing in Sully for people with tuberculosis. I hadn't been there very long when I found myself outside matron's office. I wondered what I was guilty of this time, and I was a little worried; after all I had exams to sit. I had to get my prelim, or my nursing career would end there and then. I was innocent and anyway, I decided I hadn't been there long enough to get up to much.

Standing in front of a different matron this time, my eyes riveted on the stiff bow of her cap fastened under her chin. It wobbled when she talked and so did the hat – I had never seen a hat like that in hospital before! Her expression was enough to stop me giggling under my breath. Something was obviously up. "These men can't stand it nurse, can't stand it I say, thick black stockings and a lace-trimmed petticoat." I'd been showing far too much of both it seems when stretching above the beds to reach for a thermometer. "Provocative nurse, very provocative." I was innocent – although I was fond of my broderie anglaise trimmed petticoat!

I also innocently denied putting syrup on the senior Sisters' toilet seats – although it wasn't beyond me, I must admit. Somebody else however felt desperate enough to want to keep them off the wards for just a little bit longer, and I fully agreed with that.

We returned to our parent hospital a little brighter and now quite senior, to a second year, sporting another stripe on our right arm sleeve. Life had settled down, we thought. Prelim had come and gone – we all passed that – and it was heads down for the finals now. I hoped no more visits to matron would happen again. I should have known better!

I had literally only been back five minutes when I was outside matron's door again. A whole new set of first year students had almost simultaneously been thrown into cold baths the night before, giving the oilcloth covered corridors a good soaking as well.

"But it wasn't me matron. I was out all evening." A quick check proved it. "Very well nurse, but you would have been there if you had been in," and I couldn't really argue with that. It was time for 'block' again but that never really happened as a smallpox epidemic broke out and we were all busily involved with that.

Three years had passed and we were now state registered nurses with a hospital and state certificate and a very grand prize-giving day as part of the celebrations. Was there a gleam in matron's eye as she handed over our certificates? We had had a great deal of fun and, although she would never admit it, matron had enjoyed it just a little bit as well!

Midwifery loomed on the horizon. Having qualified as a nurse in June 1963, I began the training for midwifery in Cardiff, the next September. Two of us set off. I was really beginning to flap my wings and I was now twenty-one years old.

As a result of my chapel background I had long since wanted to work in Africa. My bedroom was papered with maps and African faces. David, my brother, was training to be a chef. His walls were covered with animals and charts identifying chops and other parts of animals. Mother said she wasn't going to decorate either room again as it was a total waste of time!

The response to my now known wishes to travel, which seemed to be becoming more and more possible, went like this: "Don't be daft, Maud." "You can't stand creepy crawlies and you're scared stiff of snakes." "You've never moved far from home and what about your boyfriend?" And that was that!

6

Africa Calling

I HAVE OFTEN been asked where the interest in Africa came from. Was there a specific moment? A challenge? A growing vocation? I've always had to say no to all of those suggestions. I can vaguely remember a meeting when somebody said "Africa needs you", but that's the only instance I've been able to recall which passed through my mind.

I think it had a lot more to do with the image on the wall of the chapel, of all those different little children hand-in-hand with Jesus (the image was published by the London Missionary Society, I found out years later), together with the striking knowledge that, even to a small child, there was room for me too. The words 'follow me' were printed underneath which echoed the hymn I had heard so often: 'Follow, Follow, I Will Follow Jesus'. I was part of the picture, the little girl in a gymslip tucked away in the corner looking just like me.

I had to grow up a lot before I realized that the countries represented by the children were not the same as mine. Many of the children were not safe, not fed, not in school; many of them were dying, which was a huge wake up call to me.

Cardiff and midwifery training completed the picture. I was often working in the docks area and totally immersed in a new multicultural experience. Africa edged its way in as I listened to stories and delivered babies and looked after them.

The seed, I believe, was planted in my very early childhood, and just grew until I recognised it and did exactly what the picture and the hymn said: 'Follow Me'.

Many years later, in a tiny little bookshop, I found the picture from my childhood, and with great joy I have it in front of me today as I write these words. God, I firmly believe, is so close to us in the small, sometimes insignificant times of our lives and especially close to a small child who is just beginning to find her way in His world and with His people.

7

Midwifery, Languages
and a Big Surprise

MY FRIEND WENDY Jenkins and I left the Rhondda valley and arrived in the big city of Cardiff to begin our midwifery training. Part I passed quickly, lasting just six months and consisting mainly of long lecture periods and a requisite number of deliveries, attending operations in theatre and emergencies with the flying squad, which was made up of a doctor, midwife and pupil midwife who went in a fully equipped van to home deliveries when there were complications.

I don't remember our matron much except for her saying, "You are now grown-up and responsible and training for a second career. I don't expect to see any of you in my office," and she never did. We were much too busy now for high jinks and study-time had doubled as we only had six months before the dreaded Part I examinations. Midwifery training, like the prelim would stop there and then, if we didn't pass.

I can remember visiting one of the ward Sisters I had worked with in hospital, who had had a baby and I remember her words clearly now. "I can't believe it Maud. [Yes, *they* abused my name too!] You're so efficient and responsible that I didn't even know you were here."

Yes, fun-loving Maud was certainly still there but she was growing up too. I may have been told that I was becoming efficient and responsible – although no doubt there were still some who would have told you otherwise. There was spontaneous fun but no high jinks; there just wasn't time for that. There were wonderful moments. I still keep the photograph of the first baby I delivered and two odd gloves from the Christmas bran tub, one brown and one black. (It was part of the Christmas tradition on the maternity unit for each member of staff to contribute a small gift for the bran tub. As I was only there for one Christmas, I vividly remember my present of odd gloves!) Part I was by now successfully under our belts and we were off straightaway to start Part II. By that time I had met Pennorth.

Gwen Penn (Pennorth), Wendy and I crossed the city to begin another frantic six months. Six of us stood in front of matron – we were dressed in cornflower blue dresses, navy blue storm caps were jammed on our heads with an SRN badge pinned on the front and we were the proud owners of a fully equipped 'black bag'. We were now on the district – babies would be delivered at home! Navy blue raincoats completed the outfit and looking at each other, we burst into giggles. The larger nurses were dressed in small sizes, the small in large; some had hats on top of their heads, others over eyebrows; some raincoats fitted, others swamped those of us who were smaller. "That's enough of that," said matron, "You can swap them all around later." And we did, with some improvements.

Cardiff was not as busy as it is today, but busy enough compared to the valleys we had come from. "You'll have to ride a bike properly nurse before tomorrow or you'll be sent back to General." I'd never been on a bike in my life but I needed to be able to ride one in order to qualify as a midwife. So, the rest of us and I wobbled all over the place, eventually ending up at the city centre where the police constable was used to the six monthly arrival of 'pupil midwives', our new title. I just about made it, but I always wobbled on my bike and the brakes were none too special either. I could get away with just about anything by yelling "emergency" over my shoulder. Everything gave way as I sped past.

We hurtled down hills and around the bends. There were twelve of us now and we continued training throughout the winter. Our knees and thighs were soon blue and frozen. Fortunately, Marks and Spencer had a new delivery of knee length knickers (a female long john, I suppose). Next time we went out we were clad like tropical birds. Mine were scarlet and trimmed with black lace, just ending on the knee. They did wonders for the circulation and the morale. Matron barked her disapproval. "Hooters and sirens are sounding all over town – bus drivers, taxi drivers and any other kind of driver honking. Get them off at once. No, not now nurse... buy blue or black but certainly not red, green or yellow."

We were out all hours of the day and night in all kinds of weather. Returning to the flats we faced the dreaded supper of congealed baked beans and greasy cold kippers. "But we are hungry matron," the twelve of us protested, "up most of the night, cycling around the capital, studying." "What exactly do you want nurse?" said matron, fixing me with her beady eye. "Meat matron, just a little meat now and again." (Like Oliver Twist in the workhouse.) "Meat, nurse," matron retorted, straightening to her full height, "what do you want meat for? You stopped growing when you were twenty-one." Most of us were that and a bit more by now, and thought it was a bit much. We were fed very little meat, and so kippers and beans would have to stay.

It was Halloween and our expectation levels were sky-high as we were given the big sitting room for our party and allowed a friend each and a boyfriend as well. We decided we'd be skeletons, yes, that's what we would be, skeletons. We drew every bone in the body, something like 260. We painted them with luminous paint, fixed them on black sweaters and trousers, put balaclavas on our heads and we were ready. The music blared and we jived past matron. All inhibitions gone, we yelled, "This is what happens when you have no meat, matron." Nothing changed though. "Very good for your anatomy," was the only comment she was heard to make.

Some time later, I had a call on a dreadful windy, rain-soaked night. I was picked up by my training midwife. We hadn't got very far when her car spluttered and died. Leaping out she said, "I'll have to flag somebody down." She did, even at 2 a.m. in the morning. I watched her jump on the back of a motorbike, gas and air and delivery bag clutched to her chest yelling at me, "The patient comes first Maud," leaving me in a very bleak place. I hadn't gone very far looking for a phone box when a friendly voice said "Whatever are you doing out here nurse on your own? Jump in." The father-to-be wondered what was going on. The midwife arrived on a motorbike soaking wet, with the pupil midwife following her in a police car, warm and dry. "Trust you Maud," she said "always managing to come up smelling of roses."

'Maud' had followed me to Cardiff as well. "I'd like to call my baby after you but she doesn't look like a Maud." I've got two perfectly good names (Margaret and Jennifer, but they never saw the light of day). Maud Maund always went up on the 'off duty' roster and my mother was none too pleased at the repeated queries, "Whatever were you thinking of calling your daughter Maud Maund?" Friends I meet today still call me Maud and a lot of water has gone under the bridge since then.

On the whole, we had a wonderful time and were given lots of presents and freebies depending on where the baby was born: great hands of bananas strung across the bike after delivering a baby down the docks! Call in for coffee anytime, was the gesture of thanks following a new arrival above a local café. A box of chocolates, home-made cake, a fresh loaf of bread – wonderful, and 36 more babies safely brought into the world to add to the 15 in Part I. I was comfortably over the number required to sit Part II.

And that came around fast enough. Luckily, all the 'slog' had been done in Part I. There was still a lot of theory but everything was more practical now. However, the dreaded viva had to be sat. For me, who was never lost for words, it wasn't too bad but for some, terror struck right into the heart. A twenty-minute grilling on midwifery practice was not simple, whether you were chatty or not, but we tested each other and got ready as best as we could.

The important day had almost dawned. It was too late to do anymore catching up now. "Have a good night's rest, nurses," said matron, "and all the best for tomorrow." Good night's rest, indeed. Pennorth and I were off to see Harry Secombe at the London Palladium in *If I ruled the World*. We got back about 2 a.m., slept soundly and set off with the others for Bristol and the viva later on that morning.

The expected letter arrived just before Christmas 1964. With rest or no rest, sleep or no sleep and definitely very little meat, we had all become midwives. Midwives, at last! We had so much fun. Photographs show us larking about near the bicycle sheds in our student uniforms. Pennorth and I returned to our homes and hospitals, sadly only meeting infrequently over the years. Both of us had happy memories of great fun, boundless excitement and a wonderful sense of achievement. We set out to fulfil our new roles as staff midwives, and experience the pure joy of delivering babies on our own.

By this time, I had made a few enquiries about making my dream come true and turning those African babies and their families into real people. A letter informed me that I needed a year's midwifery experience before beginning to even think about working in Africa. So, yes, back I went to the same pre-nursing stomping ground, back to the parent hospital and yes, even back to the same matron who, by now, along with the tutors, were proud that some of their little fledglings had come home to roost.

Gone was PNS and in came Staff Midwife Maund. I still felt as if the young girl in the ghastly white uniform was peeping over my shoulder, especially when I turned up on the maternity unit – again. I had been there very briefly before, learning how to make beds (the corners had to be exact – the sheets 15 inches over the cover, pillow ends facing the wall – all tidy to the extreme, identical to covers folded neatly over chairs for the afternoon). Duvets have been popular for years now, and I must admit there's a general untidiness these days, where military precision used to reign. I rolled bandages in the nursery and I packed drums with cotton wool in the linen cupboard. I spent a lot of time there, hustled with the others to the furthest point away, as a shriek announced another impending birth. I hated that noise from the start until mothers told me years later that it was a helpful reflex rather than a yell of agony – I wasn't so sure though.

Nevertheless I couldn't hide this time, as I had before when I was an inexperienced pre-nursing student. Now I was in charge. The safe delivery of this precious little person was, for the very first time, all mine. Holding the red squealing bundle minutes later I heard the words, "You did that very well Maud" – yes, the practice of using my surname without the 'n' was back too. I crossed the threshold into a new profession with a love and tenacity which would last for the rest of my working life.

I still rolled bandages and when we were very busy, I still packed drums but now I functioned right across the board of maternity care from beginning to end and absolutely thrived on it. All those wet and windy nights delivering babies round the clock; all that study was paying off and the year went by very quickly and very happily.

Towards the end of the year I was invited to London to meet a missionary selection panel and, at about this time, rebellion had broken out in what was then the Belgian

Congo. I was met with some puzzled expressions which wasn't too surprising really. After all, people were leaving that part of Africa at a fast rate, and many had died. Now here was a very stubborn young woman who was doing her best in wanting to get in!

After a fairly strenuous verbal examination, I remember the final question well. Obviously deciding that I was not for turning, looking me straight in the eye, a person of great experience asked, was I ready to die? I was tired and fed up by now and responded much too quickly: "Of course I was." Deep down inside, I was not altogether sold on the idea, after all I was just twenty-three years old, in love with life and certainly my job and I wanted to get to the other end where I was sure it would all fall into place – early death or not (looking back now, I came very close at times, but survived to tell the tale).

The greatest problem was that I couldn't speak French, which was used for education. I also needed to learn the tribal language of Lingombe which was essential outside the classroom. I needed to speak this local language when in church or just walking around chatting to people when visiting outlying villages. The two languages were used almost simultaneously and I was in the impossible situation of not having the use of any of them. "This is very difficult," was the general opinion. "Why not go to India instead?" My total silence was the only response to that.

On a positive note, I was still quite young and had time to spare. Then a most surprising decision was made.

8

Brussels and Home Again

I WAS SENT to Brussels for a year to learn French. The language had been non-existent in my schooldays which, as I have said previously, were unremarkable. The long-awaited letter arrived just before Christmas 1965, "Can you come by January 6?" Well yes I could, but it meant racing through Christmas at home, seeing friends, saying goodbyes, leaving the family. Life was a flurry of activity.

I was ready at last to leave home for a whole year. An overnight stopover in the nurses' home had been about my limit up until then. "You'd better stay. How are you going to manage a longer period much further away if you start returning from Belgium?" But I went, and another year began.

I crossed on the ferry between Dover and Ostend. "You'll be met there and taken to the mother and baby home just a few minutes away." An hour later, and nobody had shown the slightest bit of interest in me, so clad in my Sunday best, with hat on head, address clutched in hand, I made my way to an enquiry desk and handed the scrap of paper over (no French remember). I can see the lady's expression now. Somebody who could speak English was sent for and informed me that, "You are a long way away from this address, about 100 miles or more by train, a long ride into the country. Stay on this train and don't get off until you see Mons on the station board."

I hurtled into the darkness, a little perplexed, and got

out at Mons station into just about nothing. After all it was quite late now. Nobody else was about. I approached a taxi driver who looked at my address. However it seemed that I was still a long way from my destination – about an hour's journey away. I hurtled into the darkness again through very isolated countryside with a stranger I couldn't talk to and unfamiliar with being driven on the wrong side of the road.

I arrived in the grounds of La Bienvenue, Blaugies well after midnight, passing under an impressive arch into a large courtyard surrounded by tunnels and castle walls. Now what, I thought! However I was greeted very warmly, in French of course, by a group of people who had long given up on me.

I was told much later by my employers that they had indeed wondered where on earth I had got to. "We were just going to bed Mademoiselle Margueritte when the taxi drew up with you in it. We were amazed to see that you had a *chapeaux* on your head." Nobody wore a hat in Blaugies. My Sunday best had long since welded itself to my scalp. "A *chapeaux*," they said, and a best one at that!

Having no idea where I was or who I was with, I still managed to settle and soon found that I shared a flat with two Dutch nurses who were employed, as I was, in the home beneath us, nursing the elderly, sick and mentally ill who were both Belgian and Russian. I fell into the work routine, but I didn't understand a word anybody said. After all, a lot of nursing care doesn't need words and I soon found that out. I still didn't know how I had ended up there though, when I should have been in a mother and baby home in Brussels, now a very long way away.

Some time later, I learned through the English-speaking teenage daughter that, at the last minute, a nurse was more urgently needed with old people than with babies, and the change had been made and there just hadn't been time to tell anybody. I wasn't worried – in fact I was beginning to enjoy it. After all, the last words I heard were "Write in about three months and let us know how you are getting on," and I did just that.

The letter resulted in a rapid visit by an official with instructions to 'get her out of there.' I can remember clearly the words she spoke as she left. "You were happy chatting away after only a short time and you're not upset or anxious. I don't see why you should move. It's good training and nobody else will speak French the way you do!" I was having a wonderful time, on the whole. I had experienced another Christmas and had never celebrated two Christmases before. January 7th marked the Russian Orthodox celebrations and parties began again and continued for another week. I learned to sing Russian carols and was coached in speech and writing and I soon became very firm friends with the elderly from a very different culture.

My experiences of chapel life in the Rhondda were soon heavily flavoured with another dimension: Protestant French worship and the Russian Orthodox church, their priests being frequent visitors to the home. This was all wrapped up with many excursions to the Roman Catholic church down the road.

I soon met other Dutch friends and of course there were several languages separating the English, French and Dutch. Walks in the park found us trotting along with a dictionary under each arm, trying to find the right words. That soon passed as our French began to improve. I soaked up everything I heard like a sponge, and caused some amusement with the colourful vocabulary I was picking up. I joined the community nursing team and was welcomed into each house with a glass of wine. I soon developed a taste for that and now had swearing and drinking to add to my repertoire!

I was taken in hand nevertheless. "Mademoiselle Margueritte you must clean up your language – you swear too much for a missionary and there will be no wine in Africa." There wasn't, but I still kept the taste and enjoy a glass – or two – right down to this day.

However, the year was soon over and I could, so easily, have stayed with them all. I was very fond of everybody and my unexpected excursion to an unexpected place was just wonderful. I would have loved to have had another year or so living in Blaugies, which had many advantages, such as the ability to travel easily to Brussels, Paris and many other places.

Pennorth flew over and I was given a week's holiday. We had a stupendous time: travelling all over the place together, sightseeing, and falling in love with Paris. Of course several months down the line I could exercise my French. What fun! What freedom! Pennorth was most impressed. But alas, I was on the way to somewhere else.

I did have severe bouts of homesickness as I longed to be with my family and friends back home. But I was advised to 'stick it out'. However, I enjoyed it all, made wonderful friends and returned home to Tonyrefail after a whole year away, much to my surprise and many others, I think.

9

Selly Oak, Birmingham and Africa

THE SITUATION IN the Congo hadn't improved and I was still young. "Now if you had a husband…" I wasn't thrilled with that suggestion! One's safety, it seems, was a little more secure with a man permanently around.

I joined a large crowd of both male and female students at St Andrews Hall, Selly Oak, Birmingham – all of whom were being prepared to live and work somewhere else (with the exception of me, it seemed). There was still a huge question mark over me. But I was determined: India wouldn't do and I couldn't get Africa out of my mind. Nevertheless, I was immersed in more studies. At the same time, for some reason, and from somewhere, I had developed a very loud, prolonged infectious laugh which some have described as being dirty! I hadn't noticed it to be honest.

One day I was sounding forth at the bottom of the garden, laughing loudly when the question was asked "Who is the African staying in the college?" "Oh we haven't got an African. That's Margaret." "Well! Margaret has certainly got an African laugh. You just can't send her anywhere else and the Congo is settling down now anyway." I was over the moon and for the first time I seemed on course for Africa. My French had improved somewhat and I now brushed it up with a Linguaphone course. Needless to say some of my vocabulary was not found there, but my French version was becoming more acceptable in some of the places I lived in.

In years to come I would learn more about that African laugh. What joy sitting under the stars around a small log fire, then suddenly, for no reason at all, bursting into loud infectious laughter, getting louder by the second, spreading to everybody else. My African friends told me that laughter was pure happiness and the louder and longer you laughed, the happier you were. I sounded just like them. God had given me a laugh and of course I was happy in the middle of equatorial Africa, hundreds of miles from anywhere, very happy and I laughed as long and as loud as everybody else.

I can well remember a young girl coming over to stay with us in the college to learn English, and the response she gave to some eminent visitor. Asked a curt question she scornfully replied, "Put a sock in it." There was a deathly hush. She thought that she'd done well. I knew what had happened of course, having also soaked up another language like a sponge. At least she didn't swear, and she hadn't been with elderly sick people either, so hers wasn't as colourful as my response could have been in the same circumstances.

Yes, I was going to Africa and yes, I was going into the heart of the jungle. They needed a nurse and midwife. Yet, as desperate as I was to get there, I still had another journey, still had another course of study, still had another exam to go. For the time being, however, I added another qualification to my collection, this time a certificate in African and Missionary Studies.

Three of us set off for Antwerp and the School of Tropical Medicine. Those six months produced files full of flies and snakes' heads. Somehow or other, one was supposed to be able to identify the fang that had ejected its poison into some unfortunate being, then be able to give the correct antidote. I just hoped I'd never get close enough to find out. Some time later I discovered that the dead snake, or just its head, was often brought to the hospital with the victim and that a book of pictures and drawings proved to be useful to the medical practitioners. I never felt safe, whether the snake was dead or alive.

The same thing applied to flies and deadly diseases. Flies were identified by wingspan, colour pattern on wings, length of tongue etc. I drew flies in my sleep, stared down microscopes and spent hours learning about them from glass displays. That was useful when I eventually reached the other end.

My French was useful on more than one occasion. Our class of thirty students were informed by the principal that we had free passes for the zoo as we visited so often to study snakes and flies. A crowd of us turned up at the gate and I was amazed to see them hand over a fairly expensive entrance fee. I strolled through wearing a student card. The others weren't pleased. "How did you do that?" My French was as fast as the principal's and nobody else had understood, so I soon got the fee back and we began the first of many visits. Even today, varieties of snakes and flies still spring to mind easily.

We lived in a number of rooms, mostly in attics. It was cheap accommodation and there was always a jug and basin for washing. A bath was taken on Saturdays, a few inches of tepid water, at extra cost. The meat tasted different and I ate it until I was told it was horse meat. I lived on eggs after that and anything else I could find.

We seemed to be a long way from town. We couldn't see a church of any description and being quite near the docks we were a bit out on a limb. Wandering around one day we came across the Seaman's Mission. The chaplain was a bit surprised to see three young females dropping in instead of the usual sailors, but we were made welcome nevertheless.

"I don't have much for females," he said glancing around at snooker tables and dart boards. "How about a coffee?" He was very interested in finding out what we were doing in the back streets of Antwerp, and while talking he invited us to Sunday worship.

"Do any of you play the organ or piano?" he asked. "We don't," said the other two, "but my friend does." That was me. My musical skills weren't that bad when I was sixteen, having had several years of lessons, but any talent had been somewhat neglected in the hectic years that followed. "Oh that's all right," he said, "have a go anyway." A few hymns later he was delighted. "I haven't had an organist for months. We can have a procession on Sunday."

I remember it well. I was seated at the organ playing the first hymn with the sun streaming through the stained glass windows, catching the threadbare sleeves of my suede jacket. Looking back we looked a right crew. Well, who was interested in clothes anyway? After all, in a few months we would be in tropical temperatures wrapped in a length of cotton. However, everybody else was very smart and expensively dressed. The English-speaking community of several nationalities made their way there. We three looked as if we were dressed in jumble sale clothes with scuffed shoes to round it off.

However, the service was helped by my tinkling of the organ keys and nobody seemed to mind that we looked as if we had fallen on very hard times. I never sing 'Holy, Holy, Holy, Lord God Almighty' without fondly remembering that special scene.

They all agreed that best clothes, especially shoes, would not be needed with us all leaving for the tropics in the very near future. That six months sped by and I ended up with another certificate, the biggest one I've ever had in my life!

We were very used to crossing the channel by now and we were off again, this time back home to Wales for six weeks. It was a totally frantic time. Every book I possessed: nursing, midwifery, mission and tropical, history, classics and...

Mills and Boon had to be painted with some foul smelling liquid made up by the chemist. Thousands upon thousands of pages had to be treated and this resulted in everyone volunteering to help: the butcher, the baker, the paperboy, the insurance collector, family friends and neighbours.

Soon the books were all packed into large tea chests, dozens upon dozens of them all soaked with liquid. A whole year later, I ruefully looked at the same books and every single one of them had holes right through the middle. I could hold one up and look straight through to the sky. I got used to it, like a lot of other things and soon learned to read around the holes. All that work back home, all those people back home, that mixture... the ants loved it and happily got fat on my collection of books from the time they came out of the tea chest.

Life was more hectic than usual. Last farewells, so many of them. Last party, so many of those as well. The last service was conducted by our close family friend, Ian Morrison, who was a Baptist minister and was one of our 'young people' in Salem, our little chapel on the hill. Trevor and Eirwen Jones were there too. Eirwen sang a solo in her very clear soprano voice which can still be heard today... and... then the day I thought I might never see dawned. Yes, I couldn't really believe it. I was on my way!

10

Central Belgian Congo, Africa – on the way at last!

Soon we were returning to Antwerp, leaving for Africa in the next couple of days. Then with luggage already stowed away on board ship, we were waved off by our friend the chaplain from the Seaman's Mission.

Five of us joined the seven other people on board and therefore filled the passenger area to capacity. The rest of the fairly large boat was taken up with cargo and was to be dropped off en route. The twenty-eight day sea voyage ahead looked promising with the prospect of being dropped off with the cargo for a spot of sightseeing in some places. Although we were just a few, we were treated as if we were on a luxury liner and dinner with the captain and first mate was quite an event: gold braid, caviar, seven courses – all enjoyed in a 10s. 6d. dress from Woolworths!

We visited Portugal, Las Palmas, Lanzarote and several other countries before settling down for the long journey to the Congo. A week or more of constant motion, rolling seas and waves followed. We did stop now and again but were not allowed ashore. Warnings from the other passengers were issued as we walked around the deck: "People have been kidnapped," or "You'll get lost". However the daily routine was soon interrupted unexpectedly, and nobody could have dreamt this one up.

"I've had a radio message," said the captain one bright, burning hot day. "An American pilot has crash-landed his

plane in the desert and I've been asked to pick him up."
My word! We were hanging over the deck rails when *he*
came aboard – very tall, very bronze, and very handsome,
seemingly unhurt from his unexpected arrival in the Sahara
desert.

We, that is, he and I, clicked right from the start. It
couldn't have been the Woolworths dress; it was too hot for
that. Perhaps it was the brief white shorts and by now the
very brown legs. We sat under the stars together by night and
watched the flying fish by day. We walked the small deck and
shared our meals together. I can't remember anybody else
much in those few days, but I can see him quite clearly, even
now. I can remember him giving me chocolate (perhaps it
was part of his survival rations), and the fact that the days
and nights just ran into each other. I can remember him
saying that he was coming to the Congo with me as well,
until one day the captain had another radio message. Chuck
(that's what he said to call him) had to go back to America
and a boat was in the harbour of Brazzaville, Congo to take
him there. I watched him go. I waved a white hanky, as he
did, as our ships passed each other. We would soon be miles
apart and steaming in opposite directions.

I was quiet for some time after that, and was told later
that the others were quite sure I'd get off and go with him.
Was love in the air? It probably came for a little while,
unexpectedly, literally right out of the blue onto a tiny boat
in the middle of the ocean.

Love, just a little bit perhaps, was wonderful but jail
was quite another matter. Over breakfast the captain said
we were stopping in Mauritania for twenty-four hours and
we could just go for a walk up the street as we wouldn't
need our passports for that. Five of us went down the gang
plank straight onto inches of very dirty, burning sand. The
sun was brilliant white, the heat unbearable, indescribable,
relentless and shimmering. There was a sardine factory on

our right-hand-side, with an overwhelming smell of sardine oil overpowering us. The call to prayer from Muslim minarets droned in the distance and we plodded on, up the street for just a few steps, when, a harsh voice sounded behind us, "Just where do you think you are going? Come inside."

That small cramped airless room was the local jail and without our passports we were all prisoners. "Don't you say a word" was hissed in my ear. I couldn't anyway, even if I'd wanted to, I just didn't have the breath. The relentless questioning went on: harsh, unkind, rough words and then dusk came and darkness fell...

Just as we were giving up hope, our captor changed his tactics. "Get out. You are all free to go." We didn't wait to find out why, but legged it back to the boat pretty fast. Our captain was smiling and so was our captor. "You were all swapped for everything I had," he said. "Crates of coke and boxes of cigarettes – that's exactly what you are all worth – just what do you think of that?"

11

Matadi and Kinshasa – places unknown

A FEW DAYS later our little cargo boat was anchored in the port of Matadi in the Belgian Congo. The Dutch captain and first mate waved us off, saying "You are all much too young to be going into this troubled country. We will be unloading here for three days. If you change your minds, I will take you all back to Antwerp and from there you can return home."

We were grateful for their kind concern but left the boat to be picked up by colleagues in a Landrover which soon broke down. That became a frequent occurrence in this vast country with few spare parts and no petrol stations. We were very isolated; there was not another living soul for what seemed hundreds of miles. Everything needed in an emergency had to be carried with you.

As for me, my excitement knew no bounds. I had arrived, ten years after first wishing to work in the Congo. The impossible dream of a very naïve, unprepared teenager had been fulfilled. I embraced my new, long-awaited life and jumped right in.

A couple of weeks were spent in the capital city of Kinshasa studying more essential information. I learned to plot out weight charts for newborn babies, test and examine water and make it safe for drinking. I weighed babies in local clinics (who screamed very loudly when they saw me). Outlying dispensaries had rarely seen a white face; year-old-toddlers had probably never seen one either. Visiting the local markets was a bonus and I bought the few souvenirs that I have around me even to this day. I got to know several Roman Catholic Sisters who were present on the same Health and Hygiene course. They were also getting ready to work in many isolated places.

I was greatly helped and encouraged by my new-found friends. They were lovely people who were prepared to work in the country for many more years than me. After ten years, I was told, they would return to the 'mother house' to be reunited with family and friends who could visit. My new-found friends, who mostly came from America and Canada, helped me to overcome my homesickness. It was lovely how we met up with one another in this vast country, all nurses and midwives, needed desperately after a long period of unrest and rebellion. My mission colleagues had all been posted nearer the city and its outlying areas, leaving me to go into the interior on the equator, a very long way away.

It was time to move on again, and I was clutching a government certificate this time, which enabled me to work in the Republique Democratique du Congo. I was soon leaving the city of Kinshasa, for places unknown.

12

Congo Stories

I SHALL NEVER forget the day when I was put on an internal flight for the thousand mile journey which followed the length of the Congo river. After refuelling half way and flying over dense jungle, I realised that I was the only white face left on board the aeroplane.

My French came in handy. "Yes, I was a missionary." "We thought so. Nobody else would go so far into the jungle – must be mad." "Work with me," said an African doctor sitting nearby. "We'll move on if trouble breaks out, which you won't be able to do from where you are going." The Mission Society need not have worried about me being in the wrong place in Belgium. This was the second offer of a change of route before I was anywhere near arriving at my destination.

I landed in steaming heat in what seemed like the middle of a field. I got used to these rough landing grounds eventually and called it an airport like everybody else. I had many hair-raising flights in that part of the world, which is in one of the most isolated spots on Earth. I flew all over the place in planes that had long since seen better days. I was always treated with great interest and was always the topic of conversation amongst locals.

Occasionally I was invited onto the flight deck for a chat, and the indigenous pilots always proudly told me that they had never had a flying lesson in their life. "Just picked it up from somebody else," they'd say. I was never sure whether they were winding me up! Later on, I was to find out that most skills were learned that way, so flying need not have been the exception.

I flew thousands of miles over remote areas of forest and through terrifying electrical storms. I got used to it eventually and took my cue and my courage from others around me. I must admit though that my courage failed me on one particular journey, when the previous two hours had seen us thrown about the sky, sure to fall to earth in some desolate spot. I had touched down in more ways than one, and nothing, just nothing would get me into the air again.

A voice called from the runway: "Margueritte, we'll carry on together." He was one of our African headmasters, striding quickly towards me. I couldn't slope off then, but the fact was that there was nowhere to slope off to anyway. "Come on, we're being called aboard," he said.

My leaden feet mounted the steps. Doom, I certainly felt, could not to be avoided. I wasn't far wrong, the next two hours were worse than anything I had experienced before, crashing thunder and lightning, a grey threatening sky, and a tiny plane thrown up and down, as if on a fairground ride. My companion called to me after one particularly bad dive and said, "Well Margueritte, I think we shall be going to heaven together." I was pretty sure of it at the time, although we both lived to tell the tale; that was the very worst African storm any of us had ever been through.

Going back to my first journey though, my first flight was followed by a 1½ hour trip across the river by canoe and an hour's drive through the forest in a Landrover. There were endless trees but few villages, very narrow tracks, precarious log bridges, total blackness but eventually I arrived at Pimu, which was to be my home for the next few years.

A garland of flowers over the door and a cup of tea welcomed me, but I can remember my wristwatch falling to bits on the doorstep – all too much for it, no doubt. Beaming

African faces, in spite of the night, greeted me. Then, a bath in two inches of cold water (I was soon to get used to that) and a night under a mosquito net – all firsts in a long line of experiences.

I soon settled down. I had to. There was no way that I could retrace that journey so soon. I got my bearings pretty quickly. I thrived on the constant buzz around me: hundreds of children in the primary school, hundreds of patients in the hospital and clinics, hundreds of families living around us and hundreds of very special people who were soon to become very special friends.

One time, I had been up most of the night in the operating theatre and was going to work as usual the following morning. Walking over to the hospital, my eyes almost shut against the dazzling sun, I was suddenly jerked to attention by a rough voice behind me. "You should look where you are going Margite." (My name had changed again because there was no 'r' sound in the Lingombe language. I was really confused by that. In one of the church services, the book of Luta was announced and I had no idea where that was. I found out later that it was the book of Ruth.)

For the moment though I was ordered to jump. With terror I viewed the obstacle in my path with horror. There, right across the hospital doorway laid a six foot live scaly crocodile. "What on earth is it doing here?" I asked the captor who was hoping to make a sale. "It could hurt somebody." The beast had great long yellow teeth and his huge, strong jaws were held together with the flimsiest piece of string. I had had a lucky escape and so had he, as the crocodile was eventually allowed to return to the river.

Some time later, a knock came at my door, late at night. "What on earth am I supposed to do with a dangerous thing like that?" I asked. "You could keep him in the chicken coop," my visitor replied. We did for a short while, but nobody believed us when told that we had a fully-grown crocodile at the bottom of the garden. He had a lucky escape as he too was released into the river soon after.

"You had crocodile stew today," said my students watching my face. I had long given up wondering what I was eating and ate what I was given. Crocodile, a bit like fish, turned up quite often along with monkey, wild pig and river eels.

Another day, a deathly hush descended on my usual boisterous class of nursing students. "Don't move," one of them whispered. A deadly three foot, green viper was slithering close to my hand, while I was writing on the blackboard. Contrary to all advice, I yelled and jumped and the reptile fell to the floor and slithered into the long grass outside. The boys ran after it and soon it reared its head ready to strike. A swift blow to the back of the head quickly killed it, after which it was fastened to a pole and presented to me (now rather wobbly and grey-faced), to bring back to Wales.

The class disbanded and we made for home (my home, that is). Bowls of bananas and custard were served all round (and didn't they just love custard) and much fun was had at my expense and some recriminations for my rapid response to the viper. Standing still has always been a problem, but just about impossible when threatened by a snake.

"Watch where you put your feet. If you're bitten you are dead in seven minutes. [Antidote is only given to children.] Make sure there's none in your bed or around the chair legs and always check the lamps where they often like to coil around." I carried on checking chair legs and lamps long after I came home to Wales and a gentle "Is there anything wrong Mag?" from my Mother reminded me that I was back in the Rhondda.

I never settled easily anywhere risky – which seemed to be just about everywhere in the Congo. There was green grass, green snakes; sandy paths, sandy snakes; brown trees, brown snakes. The boys looked after me all the time and did their best. But I still came far too close for comfort, yet surprisingly, I am still alive to tell the tale.

Snakes and I never got on. They were huge as well: Boa constrictors swallowed goats, pythons constricted quickly, but when fed, they were lazy and slept for days. Needless to say, one found me and that was wide awake. "You've got a python on your roof," said my fun-loving boys. The entire church meeting led by our pastor soon made it safe for me once again. You'll never find me in a reptile house, not even when dragged by children on a Sunday school trip. Snakes and I have never got on, and we'll never be friends.

On another occasion I woke up out of a deep sleep and thought that I must still be dreaming; any minute I'd wake up and find it was a nightmare. It wasn't and, as I peered through the blackness of an African night, something felt very different. I reached for my torch under the pillow and shone a faint beam of light around the walls. The walls seemed to be moving and my bedroom was getting smaller by the minute. Then my worst fears became true, the mud walls were alive with ants, millions of them all around me. They *could* eat me whole, strip my bones bare in a matter of minutes. Should I make for the door? Dire warnings sounded in my head, so I reached for a battery phone, and screamed "ants" to the person on the other end.

In a few moments my rescuer was beside me looking something like a fisherman in winter and a bank robber at any time of the year: every part of him was protected. In his hands he carried a soaking wet blanket in which I had to be wrapped from head to toe. Horrible! But, we both got out without a bite and it took the ants three days to find another home.

Other people could be seen leaving their homes at double quick speed and we learned to keep out of the way of ants. They ruled the jungle as well as us, marching along with the military precision of a well-trained army. On a trip out to surrounding villages I stepped out of the Landrover and howled with pain as razor sharp teeth bit into my feet. After that I never doubted that the half inch long driver ants ate anything in their way, including me.

After a time the pastor, trying to hide a smile, said "You'll have to stop bathing in the river Margueritte." My protests fell on deaf years and I was back to two inches of grubby cold water. Oh, how I had loved the warm, clear, pure water – a long cloth and a bar of soap. Brilliant hot sunshine and no need for a towel! I loved my frequent excursions to the river with my African friends. It was the highlight of my life. But I had to stop. Why? It seems I was totally oblivious to the large male workforce who ground to a halt and took great interest in my visits. They shouldn't have been watching me but I suppose curiosity made them look, and my outdoor baths came to an end. It was all very discrete (hence the long cloth) and all very innocent (how much more white skin was there?) viewed from a distance. Curiosity, that's all it was, but the main problem was no work got done, not on bath day anyway!

Another problem arose. "You'll have to take that third piece off your *liputa*," said my smiling pastor again. Our traditional African dress was made of about six yards of colourful cloth and a blouse or bodice. At certain times, the young girls added another piece around the waist which was pleated, tucked in and fell in folds to the ground. I joined in and was given a piece that I liked. After all, I was young as well. "Take it off Margueritte, we understand that you like it, but everybody else is waiting for the baby to come." That third piece showed that the honeymoon had taken place, the expected baby was on the way and that the cloth was ready to receive him – to wrap him in and fasten him to your back while working at home or in the fields.

The mischief and fun were irresistible but it was not

appreciated by all. Missionaries weren't expected to behave in such a way, especially masquerading as a mother-to-be when actually single!

I enjoyed it anyway and, of course, I knew what it was for – I was a midwife after all. I liked the fashion statement and was not, as some would say, 'declaring my honeymoon and its expected fulfilment'. 'Fun' and 'missionaries' didn't always go together but I am afraid that I was sometimes the exception, perhaps because I was still quite young, not yet twenty-five. I had fun and enjoyed every minute of it!

On another occasion, I awoke into pitch-black darkness that can only be found in the depths of an African night. Something or somebody was scrabbling at the mosquito netting of my kitchen window and trying to get in. Several intruders did turn up from time to time, but were frightened off before they could do much harm. Now footsteps sounded through the living room, drawers noisily emptied, cupboard doors slammed. I was terrified. Warnings sounded in my head. Don't move, don't make a sound. An intruder must not know that you are in the house.

I fumbled for my torch but the batteries were dead. Having been away for a few days, there was no oil in my lamp either. It was much too dangerous to get out of bed. I might be heard moving around or I might step on something deadly. Not long before, and not too far away (by African standards), a person had been shot dead when he tried to get help in the same situation. I froze into a huddled heap and cried out to God, "Help Me!"

As plain as any voice, back came a reply "What do you want Margaret?" I replied, "I need a light." Instantly my room lit up, splitting the equatorial darkness in two. I got out of bed and went to my window just as the bedroom door was opening.

There was an amazing scene in front of me. There was my beloved African pastor running from his house to mine in his pyjamas with a gun across his shoulders. Several others followed him and the intruders raced into the jungle.

Total mayhem confronted us all. We had few possessions but all of mine were scattered on the floor: table, desk and boxes which served as chairs all upturned, my passport missing. I can see all their faces now as I joined them unharmed. "How did you know I needed help pastor?" I asked. "You had such a bright light in your bedroom which shone all around the back of your house and it woke us all up. When we saw your light we knew you were in trouble." A flashing torch or shining oil lamp always signalled a cry for help at night. His response to my dead batteries and lack of oil was: "God was here tonight!"

"You must not stay here," said my colleagues, "it's much too dangerous." "Leave her alone," said pastor, as dawn was streaking across the sky. "God is here, there will be no more trouble tonight."

I've shared that wonderful answer to a terrified unspoken prayer with many friends who have passed it onto countless other friends, many of whom have found themselves in very dark and threatening places. We all share the same experience. God comes when you call, and God's light can overcome darkness restoring safety and protection.

After the incidents with the ants and the burglars, our beloved African pastor took matters into his own hands. It was unanimously agreed that it was too dangerous to leave me alone in my house which backed straight onto the jungle. Therefore, one quiet evening soon afterwards, a knock came to my door (nobody knocks doors in Africa, not in our part anyway, everybody walks straight in as everybody is welcome and nobody draws curtains. If you've got any closed curtains it tells all and sundry 'keep out you can't come in').

So, I looked out of my window and felt a sheer wave

of panic sweep over me. Outside was a very tall, war-painted stranger with a six-foot spear over his shoulder... and wearing the briefest loin cloth imaginable. I locked everything in sight and promptly disappeared. A few minutes later another knock came, and outside stood the same African man and my pastor. He is your protector, I was told. Let him in; he is supposed to frighten the burglars, not you. We became good friends often sharing a cup of tea late at night – and there were no more intruders.

Then one day, we had a very special applicant to the nursing school, although the boys didn't like it even though she was as eligible as them. So, Pauline, our first female student came to live with me.

I drew even closer into the world of tribal traditions. "Don't eat that egg, you won't get pregnant." "Never walk in the dark, or the tree spirits will threaten you." "Don't walk alone anywhere, that's asking for a mate."

Her friends and family all visited and soon there were hairdressing sessions in my back yard and always people to tea (so even more frantic requests home for cake mixes and custard). My indigenous language, much like French, was now heavily flavoured with the local dialect and yes, I'm afraid I started swearing again, but this time in African Lingombe.

Pauline stayed with me until she went further down the river to study midwifery and to my deep joy she was able to return and replace me when I came back to Wales.

13

More African Stories

ANOTHER TIME I arrived from the city by aeroplane to find nobody waiting for me at the airport. To my dismay, I got off the local bus to find that the school houses and villages were deserted. Without their help I could not get back to Pimu. Where was everybody? And what on earth was going to happen to me?

I was close to the dockside. There was a river boat due to leave and there were more warnings in my head. By now I had become used to unusual situations and unexpected circumstances. Here was another one that frightened me much as night began to fall.

The warning crowding in on me now was 'never travel alone' (the aeroplane posed no threat but a boat half-filled with soldiers most certainly did). Many of them were lining up ready to board. I knew I had been noticed. Who would miss me, a short white woman alone, with obviously no companion and nowhere to go? There was absolutely nobody to help or look after me there.

My worries were interrupted by a friendly voice saying "You shouldn't be in this place alone. You had better come with us." Breaking open a bottle of Coca-Cola, he helped me into a canoe alongside his companions. I took off at quite a speed across a very long river, heading for deep jungle with three men I had never seen before. However, they told me about themselves and the small crosses on their shirts reassured me. They were Roman Catholic Fathers visiting the convents and working Sisters, taking communion to them in some very isolated places. Pimu was sure to be in the vicinity of one of them they said. It was, but I didn't know then that it was a whole three days journey away.

Of course my colleagues expecting me in Pimu realised something must have happened and feared the worst. There was no radio link at Pimu but one was found elsewhere and our base in London was informed that I was missing and that nobody at that time had any idea where I could be. Needless to say I was, at that time, hurtling along forest tracks and spending the days and nights with many very special Sisters. Some were nursing like me, others were teachers, and many were African.

They fed me and gave me a bed. They brought me comfort and security but mostly, Christian friendship. Needless to say, I was enjoying myself in the deep thick forest where there was much fun and loud infectious laughter, but I was totally unaware of the worry in Pimu and the distress back home. The Sisters were a silent order except for one 'happy' hour each evening. What a time I had jiving and singing. During that hour we raised the roof: sewing machines whirred like grasshoppers, conversation buzzed and everybody was totally active, chatting, laughing and working. This was an experience never to be forgotten. One dear person was sewing roses onto a straw hat and, seeing my expression, she said "I may be a nun, and I may be alone a lot of the time, but I am still a woman!" We sung together; helped, supported and prayed for one another in one of the most remote places on God's Earth.

A week later I was taken by Landrover to Pimu, 100 miles away. What a crowd had gathered when I tumbled out of the Landrover. What a noise. What a welcome. I often think about how good these precious people were to me, saving me from a potentially lethal situation. "Trust you," was the comment of some, "always looking for your next adventure!"

Many years later, an Anglican priest said to me, when I was working in Tonyrefail, that he remembered me going missing. He remembered the fuss when my parents were told that I was missing. Again, years later, when I was working at home with a Roman Catholic colleague, I told her this story. She listened to the sombre fact that I wouldn't be alive today without all those precious people and the Fathers who rescued me from a very dangerous dockside. "Will you tell that story," she asked "when you are talking about Africa?" I always do and I always will, adding, thank God for the very special friends He sent.

Food or enough adequate food was always a problem. There were gardens in the forest and there were hunters and fishermen. Nevertheless, due to our isolation, reserves were often low. One particular day the nursing school cupboard was empty. There was nothing for the following day. What were we going to do? All the food we had put together wouldn't be enough. We all depended on rice arriving, sweet potatoes growing; corn was seasonal but fruit was in abundance. The staple diet of Kwanga was available but that just filled a hole. Hungry working boys needed fish and meat and the cupboard was bare! We talked about Jesus feeding the five thousand with very little. People were hungry then and needed food; people were hungry now and needed food. We didn't even have a little, there was nothing there. We began to pray in those long night hours, and I remember vividly what happened next:

Our Father who art in heaven
Hallowed by thy name
Thy Kingdom come, Thy will be done
On earth as it is in heaven
Give us this day our daily bread…

With those words, there was a noise outside. Night noises caused fear and everybody stayed in safety in their villages during the dark hours. The voice called out: "I've been out hunting and the pig will be rotten by the time I come back to the village. Can you use it?"

Give us this day our daily bread!

Our provider slept the night, our fires were lit and the students never knew how close they came to having nothing. Perhaps we never know either how close God is until we have nothing. We experienced a Biblical miracle and there was plenty left over.

14

Riverboats and Crossroads

THE AFRICAN RIVERBOATS were an experience in themselves. The length of the river and the time it took to travel along it, were the main reasons why we were rarely found on board riverboats. Another reason was that, as I have said, it was not considered safe, especially for lone women. The boat was the main form of transport for the army and others up and down the river.

The boats themselves were huge, like the old paddle steamers that I remembered from films. It was a floating city really, housing a huge market which was well-stocked with a variety of wild animals and just about anything else which could be sold or eaten. The boats contained the only clinic, pharmacy and bar for hundreds of miles, as there were very few roads into the forest and infrequent and unreliable aeroplanes. There was very little competition from other means of transport. This floating city brought the town to the people living alongside the river.

We were told that up to 5,000 people could be jammed into every available space on the 1,077 mile river journey between Kinshasa and Kinsingani. My colleague and I had a strange introduction to life on board, when we found ourselves stranded in Kinshasa with no aeroplanes flying at the time. Initially, we were told very sternly that we couldn't buy a ticket and we wouldn't be allowed onto the boat. Our colleagues were very worried about us attempting to travel on the boat. But, we had a huge distance to travel to get back to work. Later, we saw a lorry standing alongside the quayside with drivers that knew the Mission. They told us that they were travelling to Bolobo, the first hospital and Mission on this side of the river. We were given permission to travel several hundred miles on the back of the lorry, which did have a shaded area and seat, although for that distance it was rough in the extreme.

However, we climbed on board, and waved to several worried friends as we set off to see more colleagues in another missionary station. We hoped to catch up with the boat further down the river. Travelling the best part of the day and night, we were woken up when it was still very dark, to be told that the boat was coming up the river. We hastily threw our few things together and got into an outboard motored dugout canoe, helped by one of our pastors. We sped off into the darkness.

My friend was long-legged and, with a helping hand, managed to climb somewhat elegantly over the boat's rail. My short legs allowed for no such thing. Our pastor stood up, violently rocking the canoe, literally throwing me over the rail like a sack of potatoes to be safely caught on the other side, a tangle of arms and legs and yards of African cloth.

The captain came to tell us that we were to stay several decks down and that we were the only white people/women on board amongst thousands of Africans from all over the continent. "You can sleep the rest of the night in the dining room," he said. "I'll lock the door." There were no sheets, pillows or coverings of any sort and we had to contend with rolling beer cans noisily banging tables and chairs as the boat was rocking violently. We might have dozed with our feet under the furniture and heads on travel bags, but sleep we did not.

Later on the same day we watched women washing their clothes, their children and themselves in water drawn directly from the river by lowering empty powdered milk tins over the side and pouring it into large washing bowls. Whole families travelled together, busily plucking chickens, pounding plantains and cooking their meals in the long passageways of the boat. Some managed to pay for a swelteringly hot cabin crowded with bundles of merchandise and smoked meats, most of which would be sold in their home villages on arrival.

We saw that those without cabins (which were the majority in fact), packed themselves into gangways and rooftops, spreading raffia sleeping mats wherever they could find a space. Most of the men played cards, gathering in the bars to pass away the time. Barbers and tailors worked in the same way as they did in the villages and forests. Long-lost friends met up with each other, including some who knew us. Amongst all of this, the bleating of goats and squealing of pigs provided a familiar background noise.

This bustling city on water never seemed to sleep. There was always a hive of activity going on around us. Makeshift tables held soup, sugar, medicines and bread and huge enamel bowls of giant eels, which we often ate. Still more people joined us further up river. They brought lizards, snakes, monkeys (dead and alive), more pigs and many other saleable commodities. More children. More villagers. Was there really room for anymore? There always seemed to be room somewhere for the extra passengers.

As the boat hugged the sides of the forest, we saw herons, multi-coloured birds, monkeys swinging in the trees and water snakes following a canoe which came far too close for comfort. Several days later we got off the boat at Upoto, about three quarters of the way up the river, to the relief of our people there. I don't think too many of us had travelled that way before, if at all.

Nevertheless, we had to get back to work and at that

particular time, the non-existent four-hour flight would have kept us in Kinshasa for days. We had a never-to-be-forgotten time on board the riverboat and a never-to-be-felt again experience of the vibrant African culture on its journey up and down the river. We remembered some well-buried facts about the river. We were told that the river flows 2,700 miles from Lualaba crossing the equator twice, draining the vast rainforest nestled in the Congo basin. The river is said to be the second most powerful in the world, with the first being the river Amazon.

It has also been said that travelling up the river is like going back to the beginning of time, when vegetation covered the earth and the huge trees were king, set in the surrounding silence of an impenetrable forest. I certainly felt very close to the first few days of God's creation, wrapped in its beauty, soothed by the sunsets and slipping out of real time for a little while. For me it was a never-to-be-forgotten journey and one never to be repeated.

Many years later I was invited to speak at a missionary meeting close to home in Tonyrefail. I shared some of my now familiar stories, but unknown to me a colleague from my days in the Congo was sitting in the congregation. "You covered so many miles in such a short time and saw so many wonderful places and people," she said, reflecting on the isolation of Pimu and the need to get around using whatever means we could. We lived on one of the most remote points of the equator, and leaving the river to go deep into the forest meant that we had to travel many thousands of miles more than most to travel a short distance.

But times were changing fast in our part of the world too. All hospitals had to be registered and Pimu, although situated in total isolation, was amongst them. Education had been overlooked by the Belgian system, especially in nursing and midwifery. It was now to be upgraded by the

Russian system which insisted on a licence to practise or otherwise the hospital would be closed down. A member of the Department of Health had come as far as Upoto and, as a representative of the government, she had inspected every place on her list. But, it was said that she took one look across the river and heard about the long trip through the forest and promptly said, "I'm not going over there," thereby instantaneously writing us off together with a hundred years of faithful sacrificial medical missionary work.

A four-hour plane journey separated us from her and I travelled to Kinshasa to meet her. She was soon to find out that a five-foot-something female with Welsh *hwyl* for a backbone, and rapid idiomatic French with well-placed swear words, was more than a match for her. I visited her in the office at the Department of Health every day. In Kinshasa we shared coffee and chocolate.

But her initial amusement soon turned to irritation. Her bags were packed ready to return to Russia, as she considered her job to be done. Many other hospitals and dispensaries failing government standards were closed down. "I'm not coming," was her final threat at some point during that third week of her receiving me in her office. "What are you so worried about?" she said, followed by several derogatory statements that I only understood I'm sure from the way I had been exposed to and learned my French. The next few days saw her in front of her boss who wanted to know why she had left Pimu out of her inspection. Speechless, she was ordered back up the river into the jungle to inspect us.

When I returned from Kinshasa to Pimu, the response from the mission was that they didn't believe that she would come. However, she soon arrived and completed the inspection. It was a very good one and she was delighted with all that she had seen. The nurses could now receive their upgraded certificates and the medical work would continue unhindered into the future.

It was certainly a crossroads for all of us. I did receive a very nice thank you letter from the mission headquarters, which I appreciated. However I am more than sure that my rapid idiomatic French, smattered with relevant expletives, carried a lot of weight as well.

We had always had an excellent nursing and midwifery training school with relevant hospital buildings, pharmacy and an operating theatre together with medical surgical and children's wards. There was also a whole village not too far away where many people were recovering from leprosy. The conditions had regressed during the troubles, so keeping these services was of utmost importance. Supporting all of these was a large primary school and a very busy church, a vibrant centre of Christian witness in one of the most remote and inaccessible places on God's earth.

While I was writing about the Congo and looking back at old photographs and letters, I came across a newspaper article which was yellow and creased with age. It was dated Saturday 31st July, 1971 and entitled, 'Old man river'. The article was written by Gregory Moorhouse. He said, "There were talking drums and one of the messengers said the white man was coming up the Congo." I can only think that Mum must have kept it. The article reminded me of my journey upriver on the riverboat on this colossal river which is about 5 miles wide in places. The part of the riverbank where our missions worked, with the exception of Pimu deep in the forest, stretched from Kinshasa to Kinsangani, about 1,000 miles long.

It was H M Stanley who had opened up this particular piece of river and slice of Africa to commence the teaching of Christianity. He was closely followed by his hero, David Livingstone. His image of the Congo was similar to the one

I had: one of the great tranquil water, thick with islands of large clumps of purple weed forever floating downstream in a million pieces, of sudden storms that can turn a smooth surface into waves three and four feet high under the monsoon of a downpour, of humming birds darting from bush to bush and fireflies winking in front of you travelling through the night.

In the article I read about Bolobo (where I had been thrown aboard the riverboat), one of many settlements discovered at the riverside by missionary and explorer George Grenfell a hundred years before. His little steamer *Peace* was shipped in 800 sections from the river Clyde to Stanley Pool before she could be launched; its boiler now lies rusting in a missionary garden, a piece of Africa's Christian history.

I remembered the generosity of African culture as I read this article; the author describes how he'd been showered with gifts from very poor and isolated people. Huge hands of bananas straight from the tree, pineapples, a few eggs, always a chicken and certainly eels were amongst the many gifts given to us after a baby had been safely delivered or an operation successfully completed. For a moment I reminisced while reading the article, and cherished the memories that have survived to the present day.

*

I returned home from the Congo faster than I arrived. Receiving a letter was so infrequent; regular news from home was non-existent. When post eventually arrived, either by aeroplane or riverboat, it was passed onto just anybody who had a bicycle and it would then be brought the last hundred miles to the mission. News, when it came, came all at once.

It took months during the year I was away to discover

that my paternal grandmother who lived near us had died. The obituary notice, her funeral service and the first letter telling me of her deteriorating health all arrived together. I could remember my dear eighty-four-year-old Gran saying, "How old will I be when you come home Margaret?" and my reply "Eighty-eight Gran, I'll see you then." But it was not to be and the isolation of the forest brought shock and sadness when letters did not come in time when a family crisis was taking place so far away.

In 1971 there was no airstrip near to our settlement and no radio or any fast method of communication. A crisis led me to leave my African home without packing. I just left with my passport and the summer dress and flip-flops that I stood in. I was told an aeroplane ticket home would be waiting for me in Kinshasa. A telegram had arrived in the city for me from our London base:

Dad critically ill. Return home at once.

The same thing had happened again as it did with Gran. No news of the deteriorating health of my beloved fifty-one-year-old Dad, who had severe heart failure, had reached me. My precious Dad, such a long way away. The long journey by Landrover, canoe and internal flight took three days. The Boeing 707 which flew me to Brussels took seven hours and fifty minutes. Having been asleep for most of the night flight I didn't know where or what had hit me when we landed. The tiny plane awaiting me in Brussels had already boarded and I was waved on quickly as the engines were revving up. As I fastened my seat belt, my exhaustion and distress overwhelmed me. My rapid exit from Africa and the long journey had caught up with me.

I can remember the young man sitting alongside me on the plane very well. He was returning to London following a business trip and was amazed when he found out where

73

I had just come from. He chatted to me about my family, friends, job, and brought a sense of normality and calm back to me. I have often thought since how special it is when the right person turns up at the right time. Without his concern and company, I'm not at all sure how I would have coped with that particular journey.

No-one was waiting for me at Heathrow as nobody knew when I was returning. The telegram to my parents said, "Expect Margaret in UK in the next three days". I got to Paddington station alright; I had some English money tucked away in Africa for that purpose. The train journey through now familiar countryside took me to Cardiff and was followed by a bus to Tonyrefail. It was comparatively easy, as I had no luggage, just a purse and passport.

I arrived on my doorstep three days and ten hours after leaving Pimu, deep in the forests of equatorial Africa. I knocked on my front door in Tonyrefail in the Rhondda Valley. The journey had been a terrible shock to the system but proved to be a lot quicker than the twenty-eight days it had taken me to get there.

My parents and David were delighted to see me and so was Rex my dog (which had been bought as a gift twelve years earlier). They never did say a word, not even much later, but my appearance must have given them quite a shock.

During one visit to Kinshasa I had a photograph taken, intending to send it home. When I saw it I sat on a kerbstone and cried. I was very thin, my skin yellow and my hair was indescribable. I ripped it up there and then. I didn't know of course that my rapid exit wouldn't give me time for improvement. I arrived home looking just the same as in the photograph, only much worse, if that was possible.

When approaching furlough, workers in mission are given the time to wind down, time to pack, have a rest, and eat better food. Of course none of that happened to me as I was plucked from one situation straight into another. My skin was still a very unhealthy yellow, the years of equatorial sunshine had not turned me brown or black as my students had hoped it would. I weighed just over seven stone and was skeletally thin. Back home, two pints of extra full-cream milk went on the shopping bill straightaway.

Nursing friends, chapel friends, any friends visited thick and fast. Years later I was told that the word had got around. "Go and visit Maud – she's back and she looks as if she's dying."

My hair, always a source of trouble, was now shorn like a sheep after the years of abuse with a cut-throat razor. Hair had to be kept off the neck as globules of sweat and dust caused irritation and infection. We never possessed a mirror. Self-image was regarded as bringing bad luck and worse. So I never knew what I looked like until that photo in the city.

Now my family were facing the same image, but compounded with outlandish clothes. Where did anybody find warm clothes in an African market anyway? The solution was a long sleeved cotton shirt and trousers belonging to somebody else, and shoes two sizes too small, all from the same African market. I was frozen stiff having left the equatorial heat at great speed and arriving in the coldish temperatures of early autumn. Coal fires were soon banked twice as high and roast dinners by the dozen were lovingly prepared. But it took months of adjustment before I could tolerate any of these. Rice, sweet corn, plantains and even sweet potatoes were sourced from all over south Wales. In Africa, bread and butter were luxuries and once these were back in my diet, I was on the road to recovery.

David wasted no time and went straight out and treated

me to a beautiful brown and cream Welsh tweed coat which was all the fashion then. I wore it for years and it restored my body temperature to somewhere near normal.

As far as my feet were concerned, they took weeks to recover. Bruised, swollen and blistered, they would only tolerate Dad's size twelve slippers. I wore these when I eventually put one foot in front of the other outdoors. However our main concern for the present was Dad. I was shocked to see the change in him. There were no significant heart problems before I'd left for Africa, although we had always understood that the rheumatic fever he'd had as a child could eventually cause a problem.

Dad survived the crisis which brought me home, but now greatly weakened he faced a battery of tests and was told that heart surgery was the only solution. In those early days, surgery as such, was in its infancy and the prospect filled us with dismay. I was back now in familiar territory. Dad was nursed by friends and colleagues, X-rayed and examined by doctors I had worked with in the past.

I joined them whilst the X-rays were interpreted. I sat in on discussions with medical and surgical teams reluctantly having to face the fact that there was no alternative. Dad would not survive another crisis. My beloved father was twenty-one when I was born. My friends and I often said he was good looking with chestnut-brown hair, which I inherited, with not too many waves. Needless to say, he had a very cute overwhelming smile and a hearty laugh which was shared with everybody who came to our house.

Dad was a deacon in our little chapel on the hill and Mum and all their friends would sing around the piano, with me tinkling the ivories and David cooking supper. David always served custard slices, his specialities, which were requested at parties for years to come. Dave and I often smile now when we recall one of Dad's friends saying that he'd like an ice slice as big as a tea plate. The next time he visited Dave did indeed make a plate-sized cake especially for him. Dad always left a spare plate when laying out the meal table and whether word got around or not, somebody always came to share our meal.

"Who is Margaret's new boyfriend?" nurses sometimes asked which did his ego no end of good. We were great friends and I loved him totally. We did have a few precious days with Dad after surgery but his recovery did not continue and he died on the 23rd of December 1971.

*

The Christmas tree fairy lights and presents were all taken down and although we were supported by wonderful friends, we descended into a deep gloom as we laid our beloved father and husband to rest just as the new year started. Even to this day there are no words to describe how I felt at home with my mother and brother. Tears flowed like a river and even three years down the line, my pain and desolation had not waned. After all, Dad had called me the lodger for years, as I popped in and out during nurse and midwifery training, Belgium, Birmingham and Africa. Dad was forty-seven and well when I left home for work with the mission, and I was certainly ill-prepared to lose him aged just fifty-one.

This painful time was never spoken of, as depression set in. I appeared to be functioning and getting on with the job, but somewhere down the line I was to find out that depression is often the fruit of repressed anger. I honestly believed that I was wrong to be angry with God but I discovered that it could be harmful if there was an inability to express anger towards God. So here I was, in a cleft stick. I didn't want to nurse anybody anymore. I was let down and my resentment simmered inside and had nowhere to go.

I began to heal when I read that a battle with God is

important for all of us. God can take our anger and use it to help us through those times when it is unwise to direct it at someone else. This time of darkness came with tenacity, even though I was slow to recognise that all I had to do was hang on. It was also a time to find a capacity for new experiences, a creative space to make things anew when the world loses its familiar shape. Battered and bruised emotionally, I read again Dad's words in a letter written just before surgery. He wrote, 'Carry on with your missionary work.' The mission had granted me six months bereavement leave, a furlough to be spent with family and friends.

Mum returned to local preaching and joined the Methodist circuit which she'd be a member of for the next twenty years. David returned to lay preaching alongside his job as a baker. During the furlough period I was launched into a brand new, soon to be wonderful, world of deputation. I visited many towns, villages, chapels and schools the length and breadth of Wales and beyond.

15

Deputation

I WAS SOON being passed around Wales like a parcel. I was welcomed by many chapels and then passed onto others: out of one car and into another, travelling on buses, trains and even an aeroplane. It became a very hectic existence.

It wasn't long before I realized that I was surrounded by special people. I was having a wonderful time and after the very recent trauma, fun and laughter had begun to creep into my life as well.

I have one vivid memory of pulling into a very tiny railway station in Wales and getting off with clouds of confetti hovering about me. (And I vaguely registered a couple of men disappearing further along the platform.) The service was due to begin and the only way I was to get there quickly was by taxi. I arrived at the church during the singing of the first hymn to be met with looks of amazement from those same two men I had glimpsed on the train station platform a little earlier. "We thought you were part of the bridal party," they said. "It never entered our heads that you were the missionary."

At the time, I was yet to turn thirty and I was beginning to look much better; the yellow tinge had begun to leave my skin. I was also gaining some weight. A local hairdresser had styled my hair, which was some feat after a number of years of abuse. I had also been given some money to tidy myself up. After all, the African clothes and flip-flops were all I'd had in the years before.

The improvement must have been noticeable as I have a photo taken (probably by David) of the time. My hair was now curly and much longer. I had a wide smile, and sported a brand new black and white check summer coat. My feet had long since improved, after being jammed into too small a size sandal from an African market for too long. I remember my delight with my black shiny shoes with a small bow to set them off. I was told that I was quite smart, all in all!

Another picture springs to mind too. I knocked on the door of a terraced house and was met with a blank gaze, with no recognition whatsoever. The question "Can I help you?" confirmed my initial hunch. "I'm Margaret the missionary. I've come here to have lunch with you." "Good heavens!" was the answer, followed by, "Come on in, come on in." "The missionary is here – wait till you see her." Missionaries and ministers who had visited before had all needed an afternoon nap after enjoying a full Welsh dinner. "Oh no!" they said, quickly getting rid of shawls and cushions. "We'd much rather chat to you." And if I remember correctly the topic of conversation was always, "Shouldn't a young girl like you be married?"

I loved every minute of my work in deputation. There were so many caring strangers looking after me, welcoming me into their homes: a hot-water bottle in my bed, feeding me, including me in their family life. It was a very special time of meetings, conferences and youth clubs and a fortnight in Guernsey was certainly a lovely experience.

There was also the added joy of being able to return home to Mum and David in Tonyrefail whenever I wanted. However home was still a strange and unfamiliar place without Dad greeting me at the door. Two years after his death his loss to me was as raw as the day it happened.

Two phrases spring to mind, 'God is big enough to absorb your anger.' Yes I was angry. Ten years of just popping in and out of the house, for very short periods of time made me feel short-changed. The other one was, 'Consider how fortunate you have been. You have fulfilled your dream. Countless faithful others have never had the chance to do that.' I continued working and I picked up chapel life, but his loss to me at that time was so painful that I was almost functioning in automatic gear.

Then I remembered a very special gift I had been given just before I left Wales for the Congo. During a farewell service some years before, I was presented with a handcrafted single-bed size, gold-coloured quilt. On the other side was a full-sized map of the Belgian Congo. I was told that the quilt was woven by a young woman some years before, who was preparing to work in the Congo, but became ill and was never able to go. Would I accept the quilt as a gift, as I was going to follow the same route as she had longed to go?

During the time of Dad's death, I hugged that quilt close, ran my finger along the route of the Congo river, recalling the hundreds of faces and experiences that made the quilt come alive to me. As my tears flowed, I realized that I had been very fortunate, receiving a great deal more from God than I was prepared to be grateful for, at that particular time.

I remembered the short life of the young person who had made the quilt with great love, with Africa calling to her with every stitch. I remembered my beloved Dad's hearty laugh and his final written words to me. 'Carry on with your missionary work.'

The mission I was working for requested that I might like to donate the quilt (which is now quite old) to their museum. My answer was brief. "Sorry, but no." This quilt was part of the fabric of my life, and I would leave it to the museum in my will. Many years later it still stays close to me. I put it over my bed regularly. I run my fingers along the river, mentally stopping off at the many villages and always remembering the deep love that was poured into every stitch.

I began to heal. My pain decreased and I found that I could thank God, even praise God, for a wonderful Christian Dad who was so proud of his missionary daughter and Baptist pastor son.

Other memories of wonderful Christian support and friendship were brought to mind during this same period of time. Before we left for Africa, chapels and churches, work places and a huge network of friends requested prayer cards which were published by the mission. I have one with me today which I fondly look at, along with the quilt.

And here is a youthful twenty-something, smiling out from an oblong piece of cardboard alongside a map of Congo and chosen Biblical texts. I was always so surprised to see me looking out onto other peoples' lives and being included in the prayers and worship of so many friends and families.

Quite recently, more than forty years after I'd returned from the Congo, I received an unexpected package in the post. The letter inside said: 'My mother died recently and in her Bible we found your prayer card. We thought you would like to know that you were prayed for over many years and thought you would like to have your card back.' I was totally overcome. It had been tucked into the pages of someone's Bible in such a personal way and for such a long time. The pensioner now looks at the youthful girl, full of adventure and enthusiasm and catches more than a glimpse of herself as she travels the same road, but now as a senior citizen.

There hasn't been much change really, although a lot of water has flowed under the bridge since those early days. There have been times which have brought deep sorrow and disappointments but also times which still bring days of enjoyment, new experiences and a whole new crowd of friends.

But at this stage of my life, deputation was coming to an end and my tea chests were now packed ready to return to Africa. Then, one unforgettable day, a letter arrived in the post saying that major changes were now taking place. There were rebellions and great instability in the country. The Congo had now become Zaire and the educational systems were changing rapidly. I had been teaching (passing on skills) but I had never qualified to teach nursing and midwifery in Africa.

The government needed a tutor, said the letter. You are young and at home. So, you can apply to the training boards for possible further education. The pilot scheme for training midwife tutors was to take place in Newcastle-Upon-Tyne and the boards threw up their hands in horror when they found out where I'd been for the past few years. Nevertheless they gave me a try and I returned to my old student midwifery school, to my previous tutor who was exceptionally kind to me and acted as my invigilator for the theoretical exams I needed to pass. Even though I say it myself, I did quite well and, in their own words (the board's, that is) I couldn't really be turned down.

16

Up North

"IN MY FATHER'S house there are many mansions," said Jesus. I often remembered those words when the next year saw me living in a number of different places and in a variety of situations. I sincerely hoped that any contribution I might be making to a heavenly mansion would be an improvement on the earthly ones I was passing through at the time.

"I hope you will be very happy here," said my future landlady depositing a tray of tomato sandwiches and tea on the table in front of me. I didn't see why I shouldn't be. It was a nice big room, right on the street and close to the polytechnic. "Thank you," I said. "Everything is just fine." But, as I switched on the gas fire I heard a crack, but didn't pay much attention to it, until I reached for another sandwich and quickly met with the floor, eyeing the broken wood of the chair with some dismay.

The next few weeks were disastrous. Of course, the bookshelf would take all my new books. Of course it didn't, the whole lot collapsing on the floor in clouds of dust followed by colourful threats from downstairs. "That coffee table looks wonky," said one of the girls when they came back for tea – that was soon in pieces as well. But the crowning crash that nearly finished it all and nearly finished me came when I was innocently studying under the light of the chandelier hanging high up in the old-fashioned dome of the ceiling. Following another ominous cracking sound, I was very suddenly splattered with glass as the chandelier swayed and circled, bringing down glass, wood and a fair chunk of the ceiling. Staring at the hole above, I told the owner that I'd have to find a room somewhere else (after all there was not much left of this one).

The bed had long since reached the carpet too. Those legs gave way as well, some dark, quiet night. I didn't wreck the place; it gradually wrecked itself around me. I think the owner was glad to see the back of me and so was I glad to see the back of it. I wasn't the only one, just the last to go. But, where to? That's another story.

"This is the only one I've got," said the harassed clerk behind the desk, "You can take it or leave it. Please yourself." I had to have a bed so I took it, dragging my weary feet and far too much luggage (nearly all books) up far too many flights of stairs. I was soon fast asleep, only to wake up hours later to find a strange face on the opposite pillow. "I'm just passing through," she said, and was soon gone to be replaced by many others. There were someone else's clothes in the wardrobe and someone's shoes to trip over. Nobody had told me that it was a transit room with dozens of people passing through, and I lost count of the number of room-mates I had. It was a miracle that I passed the examinations. The dark shadows under my eyes must have roused some sympathy and no doubt contributed to yet another move.

"There will be no more people in the middle of the night," said the now friendly clerk. "You will be much better off in the bridal suite." Anything would be better I thought, hauling my luggage behind me and closing my door to blissful solitary peace. It was a long time until Saturday, when I had to vacate my little room for the bride's use for the day. "You can't come back until three o'clock," I was reminded as I left the building at eight in the morning. I wandered around the shops: another lingerie department, a coffee, more clothes, a newspaper, more lingerie (I don't know to this day why I bothered with silks and lace, a student grant wasn't up to it anyway. It was probably a bit of the woman struggling to get out after years without shops and frills). I eventually settled for the library, and at the end of the day made my way back. "Go away," hissed the clerk, "the bride is still there."

I lost count of the number of brides who used my room, and the number of times I wandered the streets. I longed for my own space, but I was banned, in exile at least until all the finery had gone. Weddings and I definitely fell out. The year passed quickly and I now had a midwife teacher's diploma to add to the rest.

God had yet another purpose up His sleeve and if I could possibly have had a glimpse into the future, I would have found that it held the biggest surprise of the lot. In Newcastle-upon-Tyne it was suggested to me that I attended the local Baptist church, as I'd have a very warm welcome there. I did just that, but I had dire warnings from my course tutor, "Don't tell anybody, only the pastor that you haven't long come back from Africa. You'll be worked off your feet and your studies won't stand a chance." I took the advice.

I had a wonderful year in Newcastle-upon-Tyne. Many thought that I would stay there much longer. And, at the time I would have liked that. I'd soon gained many lovely friends who looked out for me, and, as I lived in the YMCA I enjoyed lovely meals and Sunday lunches and wonderful Christian fellowship. I survived most of the exams, which were horrendous and accelerated my migraines which put me in a darkened room from time to time. The exams were demanding and difficult. Our training as midwives was painstakingly thorough, added to which we had to be trained as teachers, which was a whole new ball game.

"I think it's time to introduce you properly now," said the minister. The annual meeting and party were coming up. "You can be the speaker," he said. The total surprise on more than a hundred faces when I stood up to speak was memorable. Why on earth didn't you tell us? Why on earth didn't he tell us? Glaring at the minister, the long lists of where I could have gone and what I could have done were quickly made by the members of the church. However I did stay for a while longer and shared my overseas life with them. I left Newcastle with yet another large certificate. This time: a midwife teacher's diploma.

The longing to return to Africa was acute. However my distress and disappointment was overwhelming when I realised my health was preventing me from doing so. I was experiencing debilitating migraines and my eyesight was deteriorating and the lack of medical facilities in Africa would, as a result, be an issue.

17

Back Home Again

I RETURNED HOME to Wales to work as a midwife. Meanwhile my employers found out about my teaching certificate. Goodness, what a fuss! I changed uniform twice, and then into a suit. My salary changed three times and the wages department was thrown into a state of chaos.

I didn't want to enter a long complicated teaching programme. I just needed some cash and to get well for the future. However I was promised a multiracial class which was almost as good as being abroad. I was thrown into a whole new experience and, dressed in a suit, I prepared for a major career change.

Some years later I went to see *Joseph and his Technicolor Dreamcoat* in the local theatre. I thought about the story of Joseph and the way his brothers treated him, selling him into slavery. He was thrown into prison but eventually became governor of Egypt.

His starving brothers, who had previously hated him, unknowingly stood before the governor/Joseph asking to buy grain. God had told Joseph in a dream when he was a young shepherd boy that this would happen. When the dream came true he was completely stunned. My dreams seemed impossible when I was a young teenager, but the same God made my dreams come true too.

After being plucked from the Congo with no real goodbyes, nor a winding down period, and then being plunged into the darkness surrounding Dad's illness, I often felt that life was over for me. When the tears flowed and the yearning increased, I remembered Joseph and his dream and Africa and my dream. I remembered the first baby I delivered in the stillness and blackness of an African night, a flickering oil lamp shadowing a larger family sleeping under the new mother's bed. My reaction was just the same as the people of old, "How did this happen?"

I also remembered that I had been lucky and experienced more than most. Perhaps I had experienced only a few short years, even though I had written 'a lifetime' on the mission form. God had been faithful every step of the way, although it didn't feel much like it at the time. Life was not over, even though I felt it was: in fact a whole new beginning was just around the corner.

Soon I faced my multiracial class on the first day of their midwifery training. "What made you choose a small midwifery school on a Welsh hillside?" I asked. "Well, we had lists to choose from, closed our eyes, made circles with a pin and then jabbed and yours was the one that came up." So my days with the students began and their days in the Rhondda got off to a good start. They were the first of many students to pass through our course and came from Jamaica, Hong Kong, Mauritius, Barbados and America, together with students from England and Wales, brightening our days with unexpected fun.

"Can we go outside?" they asked me, on a very hot summer's day. Out we all trooped with anatomical dolls, textbooks and plenty of juice, but we were soon to be joined by a flock of sheep. "Teaching them as well are you?" quipped a passing doctor. Then there was a call to the labour ward and a few more births to observe, when theory turns into practice. Tears often came, especially from the new students. There was nothing quite as wonderful as hearing the first newborn cry and all students (I found anyway) reacted in exactly the same way, even though they came from all over the place.

Unbelievably to me, I was back treading the same corridors. Was this really me stepping out past the same linen cupboard, seeing in my mind's eye a very apprehensive 16-year-old pre-nursing student packing drums? Yes, it really was and the time in between had certainly brought a few changes with it.

Many new relationships were also born alongside the hundreds of babies on the labour wards. "I'm getting married," became a common announcement and all of us celebrated by taking the bride-to-be on a trip to London – Madame Tussauds, the chamber of horrors – not a reflection of things to come we hoped! We boated on the river, raced around the shops, visited the Tower of London and the highlight of the day was tea on the top floor of Harrods. While waiting, a couple of us would sneak off to buy the communal wedding gift. That became a regular routine. The sometimes delicate gift would be carried gently home resplendent in a green and gold Harrods shopping bag. What a time we had. But, everybody was waiting for my wedding! And up to my eyes as I was, the 'glow' simply hadn't rubbed off on me – not yet anyway.

David, my brother, was by now an accomplished chef and had added cake decorations and icing to his skills. "Of course Dave will make the wedding cake." That was part of the package along with a boat trip and a skate around London, Harrods and wedding dresses. He made several and for weeks patiently modelled numerous roses to decorate the cake to the bride's colour of choice. I can see his face now when one friend in particular was to marry a farmer. "Do you think I could have pigs instead of roses?" she said. "It will be a nice surprise as he is a pig farmer." Even David's skills were stretched there, but when the special day dawned, there was a wonderful cake in the centre of the table with, you've guessed it, pigs instead of roses. The upper tier of the cake was carefully wrapped up and put away for the christening. When that day arrived, Dave touched it up and replaced the roses (and pigs) with babies and cradles.

What a carry on! And not just weddings, as by now I was close to a special celebration – a milestone birthday. My, how the time had flown, and yes, I had a trip, a present and a party – but no bridegroom – as he hadn't turned up yet! I began to love my new world of students and babies. My heart was thawing out (it had taken a long time), and I was now at a respectable age immersed in a variety of activities.

*

Africa was still very much to the fore. Everybody everywhere loved the stories and they were all woven into the fabric of my life. They helped to make me the person that I am today and gave me the loudest laugh anybody has ever heard anywhere. I even surprised myself when I remembered the laugh, "It's African – send her out." It got louder out there – and reminded me that, as it resounded out, it let everyone far and wide know that life was wonderful. Yes, in spite of everything, I was happy, I was satisfied and life was fun again.

If I could learn that lesson in Africa with beloved friends who were ill, poor and living in war zones, then it was time I settled down and, although Africa would always be my first love, it very much appeared that home was certainly the place, at that moment, for me to be.

The chapel I had grown up in was still there, but my parents had moved house in the intervening years and likewise moved chapel. I joined them in between shifts, babies, programmes, the singing group and trips out. One day I needed to see the vicar of the parish and was told to find him in the church. I did just that and years and years after my christening in church, I returned to *their* fold.

Life took on another dimension, and again there were new people and new activities. My morning visits to church influenced me right from the start and it brought many different strands of my life together. Mum joined me a few years later; David was now married with a small son and stayed in the Baptist tradition. And after many adventurous years and lots of surprises, I couldn't even begin to guess what God had up His sleeve next.

My one year's teaching stretched into two and I suppose having been given the gift of the gab, as some would say, I joined the hospital radio group which was in the maternity wing. After attending several short radio courses I ended up in what had previously been a broom cupboard. It housed a fair amount of broadcasting equipment and my first two-hour programme entitled *It's a beautiful world*, was soon off to a rollicking start.

Of course I had a captive audience in the hospital. What a riotous time we all had, jammed together for interviews, with some participating out of sheer curiosity. Telephone requests for a favourite record soon rolled in. Arriving for my usual session, I passed a porter who didn't usually work on Saturday mornings. "What are you doing in?" I asked as I hurried past. "Oh, I always listen to *It's a beautiful world* and I sometimes win a prize in the competitions." It was very flattering to know that he enjoyed listening to the programme.

I have a lovely picture in mind when a fairly serious-minded doctor came to visit the broom cupboard. Amongst many things, he told the quite large invisible audience that he played the violin as a boy, a fact unknown until then. Well radio, even in a small area, can be powerful. The next time he did his rounds on the wards, he found all his patients in bed and all the ward staff playing imaginary violins on the way. "I'm not telling you anything ever again," he hissed, when we were together in more formal circumstances as midwife and doctor. From that day to this, hospital radio has always played an important role in my life.

Many years later, when I worked in other areas of the hospital, people still recognized my voice. "I heard you as I woke up from my anesthetic, Margaret. You cheered me up, and I loved the music." Or: "You must be Margaret. I knew your voice straightaway." I loved every minute of it, jamming programmes between lectures and babies. The students loved it too, often being on the receiving end of a prize – which was a special bonus at the time.

Over the next twenty-five years I became a regular visitor to BBC Wales. Lots of my stories have been very popular, with total strangers phoning up, writing letters and sharing the fun. One day I was asked if I would like to train with the BBC. I was very surprised and jumped at the chance. I was told that I'd have to start at the bottom. That was fine, a change of career! I was told to think about it or to continue to be freelance which is what I still do to the present day. I wrote and contributed to 'Pause for thought', a religious spot on the radio and continued to participate in many other areas of radio. I am very comforted by the fact that so many others, at night at home or in their cars, in many other countries too, have shared in what God can do in their lives. At ten years old, God's faithfulness reached into me and stayed with me in the rollercoaster of experiences and places in which I found myself in life.

I remember the reaction of phone calls and letters which I received when sharing the 'scatty' nurse and midwife stories, the thrills and spills of the Belgian Congo, student life with me as the teacher this time and then, several months later, sharing the news that God had another change of direction planned for me.

I often wonder how different life would have been if I had started on the bottom rung of a new career path in radio. Life for me was changing again and unbeknown to me, moving in a completely new direction. While I was working as a midwifery tutor (which stretched over ten years), I became an examiner for midwifery and a trade union representative. At one time, I was away at a conference embracing both these roles when the topic of retirement was discussed. I was interested, but horrified when I became part of the conversation which included flowers and weight reduction. You can earn a lot of money, I was told, boost a pension.

Most colleagues present knew that I had only been a salaried worker for the past ten years. Later on I mulled this over and this is what I said, "Dear Lord, deliver me from flowers and calories! When my retirement comes, You will have to handle it." I should never have said the words! Meanwhile life went on with many different experiences. Teaching in hospital, students, friends and chapel life flowed together in a happy companionship.

18

The Reflectors

TEACHERS, MIDWIVES AND many students met together in the nurses' Christian fellowship every Thursday evening for an hour followed by light refreshments. We were often joined by visitors and staff passing by the open patio doors; sometimes by patients too, who were able to walk from the nearby wards. I thumped out choruses on the piano and was joined by Edna and Chris on guitar. Our overseas students provided harmony, new songs, tambourines and hand clapping. We were a noisy, joyful group and were soon invited to local chapels and churches.

"We need a name," was suggested by one member one evening some weeks later. Edna was looking at an electric fire at the time and it reflected light and warmth into the room. "How about 'The Reflectors'?" she said, "reflecting the love of Jesus." Reflectors we became and we were soon sharing Christian fellowship all over the place. We had a wonderful time together and the group continued for many years with our lives going along different paths that none of us could possibly predict at that particular time.

One of our students was about to be married, the first in our Reflectors group. The exams were behind us as talk of wedding dresses, cake and honeymoon took over. Eventually the wedding preparations seemed to be ready, with the Reflectors booked to sing during the signing of the register. When we passed in the corridor not long before the wedding, I asked if everything was in place. My simple query was met with a distressed wail. "The organist can't come and there is nobody else to take her place. Will you play for me?" came the most disturbing question. I had thumped out choruses and hymns on a piano (I hadn't done too badly in the Seaman's Mission many years before) and in the African jungle there was no organ or piano anyway. However, her long face and acute distress prompted me to say that I would have a go. At the practice run I was faced with a new electronic model with a variety of stops and foot pedals. I frantically pressed several knobs whose purpose I didn't understand, achieved a reasonable sound and ignored the foot pedals which I couldn't reach anyway. Her vivid smile and a huge sigh of relief left me with no choice. It was too late to turn back now. The big day arrived all too soon. I switched on the organ and, with a nod from the minister, one of my students came up the aisle to my very nervous playing. "It was lovely," she said, although I wasn't quite so sure.

The Reflectors, all fifteen of us including Mum, were resplendent in wine and cream long skirts and cream blouses, all smiling broadly along with the bride and groom. We were captured in the wedding photographs taken after the service. It was a wonderful day and a tape recording of the service did reassure me that the electronic organ wasn't so bad after all.

A few more stories come to mind. Vi, a midwifery and Reflector colleague, with a good soprano voice, often took a solo spot when we were all performing together. "Yes, we have a piano," was the response to my question and "Yes, it's in good condition" was a frequent reassurance at the venues where we held our performances. On one occasion we turned up to a little chapel in our brightly coloured skirts and blouses and were welcomed by a friendly crowd. I was taken to the piano with upturned cover and arranged several sheets of music. Glancing at our group, who were

With my brother Dave. I'm three and he's a one year old.

My mum and dad as Christian Endeavour presidents at Salem English Baptist Chapel in Tonyrefail.

Now aged five in 1947.

The image which inspired me all those years ago. A poster from Sunday school of Jesus and the children. I thought that the little girl in the gymslip looked just like me.

Training to be a midwife in July 1964.

Gwen Pennorth and me larking about during our Part II midwifery training.

My fellow student nurse colleagues at East Glamorgan Hospital, Church Village, 1962.

The first baby I delivered in 1965.

7

VISAS

TRANSPOSITION.

Visa d'établissement
– à durée indéterminée ;
– à durée déterminée.

N° 0584 8/421/68/D.233.605

Le présent visa doit être utilisé endéans les trois
mois de sa délivrance, sous peine de péremption.
Il autorise le séjour de titulaire pendant une pé-
riode : INDÉTERMINÉE DÉTERMINÉE, pre-
nant fin :

le .... 19 ......
– à l'expiration du contrat.

Fait à LONDRES le 24-7-68
Par délégation
(timbre sceau) P.C.C. Kinshasa, le 15-9-70

DDI   Administrateur du C.N.D.
                         Ph. KOMANI
                         CAPITAINE

CERTIFICAT — GETUIGSCHRIFT   3107

Conformément au décret du 19 mars 1952 et à l'ordonnance n° 71/392 du
20 novembre 1952, il a été procédé à la vérification des titres de

Mademoiselle MAUND Margaret Jennifer

né le BRIDGEND à BRIDGEND , Angleterre
gebores de   te

Ces titres remplissent les conditions requises pour l'exercice au Congo

de la profession de

INFIRMIERE-ACCOUCHEUSE.

Kinshasa, Le 10 décembre 1968

LE SECRETAIRE GENERAL,
NZ NGANZU

Valediction service in 1968 prior to my
departure for the Congo.

My visa and work permit allowing me to
work in the Congo.

A prayer card for my service
in the Congo.

FIELD OF SERVICE

I am crucified with Christ, nevertheless I live; yet not I, but Christ
liveth in me, and the life I now
live in the flesh I live by the faith
of the Son of God who loved me,
and gave himself for me.
Gal. 2.20

I can do all things through Christ,
which strengtheneth me.
Phil. 4. 13.

READY TO DO WHAT SO
EVER MY LORD THE KING
SHALL APPOINT.
2 Sam. 15. 15.

CONGO

EUROPE

AFRICA

Headquarters G.B. B.M.S.
93. 97. Gloucester Place,
London W 1.

FIELD ADDRESS
Smith Thomas
Memorial Hospital
EBMC. BMS. Pimu
par Lisala
Rep. Dem. du Congo

HOME ADDRESS
'Charis'
52, Llantrisant Road,
Tonyrefail, Porth,
Glam. S. Wales.

MARGARET J. MAUND   SRN. SCM.
SERVING THE LORD
with the
BAPTIST MISSIONARY SOCIETY
in the
CONGO   68 - 71

27 MILL ST
TON
CF 39 8AB

The boat which took me
from Belgium to the Congo.

A photo taken whilst I was
living in Pimu. I'm dressed
in the Congolese *liputa*.

Women and children living
in Pimu village.

Travelling with colleagues between villages.

Primary school children playing a much loved game of football.

Student nurses practising their skills outdoors.

A baptismal service.

Playing a talking drum.

Pimu Church.

Visiting Kinshasa to pick up nursing certificates.

Primary school children in Pimu.

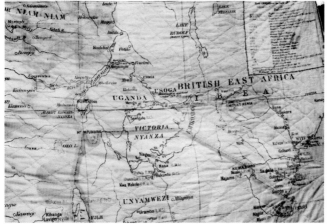

The embroidery I sent home as a Christmas gift to mum from Pimu in 1970.

A quilt made up of the map of Africa.

On my return from Africa and about to start work in deputation.

The Reflectors
singing group,
with mum holding
Candy, the poodle.

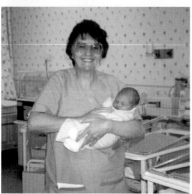

Life as a busy midwife, working all
hours. I delivered my last baby in 1993.

Last night at work: my farewell party in the
early hours of the morning.

At the turntable doing hospital radio in Aberdare.

Please pray for those to be ordained this Petertide

including

Margaret Jennifer Maund

who is to be ordained Deacon

by

Roy, Lord Bishop of Llandaff

in Llandaff Cathedral

on Saturday, the 25th of June 1994 at 10 a.m.

Pray also for her Mother, Brother and Nephew and the Vicar and people of the Parish of Cymmer and Porth, where she will serve

27 Mill Street
Tonyrefail, Porth
Mid Glam. CF39 8AB   **Telephone 670085**

Prayer card during my ordination as a deacon in 1994.

With mum and Roy Davies, Lord Bishop of Llandaff.

New Year Brings First Women Priests to Wales

Margaret Maund who serves the Parish of Cymmer and Porth is to be among some of the first women in Wales to be ordained as Priest!

Margaret Jennifer Maund is to be ordained Priest by the Very Reverend Roy Lord Bishop on Saturday 11th January in Llandaff Cathedral. First mass will be held in St Johns Church in a united parish celebration on 12th January at 10.00 am.

Newspaper clipping from January 1997, when I was one of the first women to be ordained a priest in Wales.

Dressed in my black cassock and cape.

Reverend Margaret Maund will never forget her years as a missionary in the heart of Africa

Vivid contrasts between jungle life and the Rhondda

WHEN you've had to survive on monkey meat and python piri piri in the jungles of Africa, life in the Rhondda valleys can hold few fears.

Reverend Margaret Maund encountered these and other experiences during her four years as a nurse and midwife in Zaire, formerly the Belgian Congo, in two spells through the 1960s.

And she still sees herself as a missionary, even though she's back in the relative civilisation of South Wales.

Juggling two full time jobs is never easy and Margaret finds herself leading a a double life as a priest and a nursing sister, making frequent quick changes from her ecclesiastical robes into her starched white uniform.

The two roles overlapped this week when she was granted permission to celebrate Mass at the nursing home where she works at her lay job.

Margaret, who often works day and night duties, can survive on very little sleep.

Tiredness has never been a problem in her high octane existence.

"I can kip on a bus quite easily," said the Reverend.

"Being able to drop off to sleep anywhere is what keeps me going."

Margaret, 55, was one of the first women priests to be ordained in Wales and she is curate of Cymmer and Porth, carrying out her non-stipendiary Ministry at St John's in Cymmer and St Luke's in Llwynypia.

When not carrying out her religious duties she works as a nursing sister at Rhiwfelin Nursing Home, near Tonyrefail.

"The hours are long," she admits, "but the two jobs mingle so well.

"I don't feel there is very much of a division between nursing and pastoral work and I'm so pleased to be able to come back to the nursing home when I am off duty to celebrate Mass and have a good old sing song.

"I'm often told I'm far too noisy to be a Minister, but it comes from my time in Africa when you had to shout to be heard over the sound of the drums."

Margaret wanted to be a nurse from the age of 14.

She trained at East Glamorgan Hospital and the maternity unit at Glossop Terrace in Cardiff.

The job proved to be the inspiration for her later travels.

"Delivering ethnic babies opened up a whole new world for me," she said.

"I'd never been any further than Cardiff before, but I developed a bit of a wanderlust."

In Africa, Margaret became one of a team looking after 10,000 people in what could best be described as the middle of nowhere, braving electric storms in planes piloted by people who had never had a flying lesson, to reach communities spread across 15,000 miles.

"They didn't have much, but the hospitality was overwhelming," she revealed.

"They shared half of everything and because it was a very vital half, you never refused.

"We ate everything from sweet potatoes, to fish, developed reptiles like crocodiles and snakes.

"Because it was so highly spiced, you were never quite sure what it was.

"One Christmas – because there were 400 of us to sit down to dinner –

MISSIONARY: The Reverend Margaret Maund says Mass at the Rhiwfelin Nursing Home near Tonyrefail.

PICTURE: Paul Rose

'Our food was so highly spiced, you were never quite sure what it was'

INTERVIEW by Jenny Longhurst

we had permission to shoot an elephant because it was the only thing that would have been big enough to feed everybody.

"But nobody could bring themselves to do it.

"I'm vegetarian now. I can't bear the thought of eating animals."

Jungle life also brought its fair share of hazards, not least of them the ants which teemed in the walls of her mud bungalow and the snakes, often to be found lurking in and around the bed.

"We had to strip our beds down every night before getting in," said Margaret.

"The ritual became so ingrained I did it for two years after I came home, even though I wasn't really expecting to find a python in the Rhondda."

In the end, Margaret's mother became so puzzled by the ritual that she asked her if there was anything wrong with the bed.

One of the worst aspects of her life in Africa was having to work through the pitch black nights, with only paraffin lamps for light.

The strain eventually affected her eyes and frequently brought on violent migraines.

But despite her trials and tribulations, Margaret has fond memories of her African adventure.

"African joy and spontaneity made a big impression on me and has stayed with me," she said.

"The Reverend is still very much a missionary and there is a lot of joy and love in the nursing home, even though people are here for the remainder of their lives."

Margaret the priest has never been a banner waver for the ordination for women.

But she told the Echo: "Once the Church was happy with it and the need was there I felt it was right.

"It's made so much difference to me.

"I have a feeling of being complete.

"I intend to carry on with the two jobs for as long as possible.

"The whole of my faith seems to have come together, especially in the caring of the sick."

Full page feature in the *South Wales Echo,* June 1997. I often changed my uniform from nurse to priest in the same day, and sometimes in the same shift!

Joybells performing.

My mum's 90th birthday, with my brother Dave and nephew DJ.

My great-nieces Caitlin and Courtney.

And finally, my favourite Robin!

now all in place, Vi prepared to start the evening with a song. Standing alone amongst the seated group, she waited for a note from me at the piano. At the time I was trying to find a note anywhere on the piano. Black, white, sharp or flat, it made no difference as Vi waited, telling the congregation, "I haven't got a note!" None of us had one! I replaced the cover, gathered the music together and joined the group. We had a lovely time and sung with gusto unaccompanied. Nobody ever referred to the dreadful condition of the piano and I was more careful checking instruments afterwards.

Another time we travelled quite some distance in a convoy of cars, arriving at a church about ten miles distant from our base. As usual, the programme was checked and all Reflectors were in the correct places. Wherever we went no one was left out. On this particular occasion I arranged my music which consisted of several sheets and books. Hands were poised ready to start. For some reason or other, a lady in the congregation decided to go through to the vestry, and caused a great gust of wind which sent every sheet of music and book flying to the floor. Fifteen pairs of startled eyes turned to meet mine. Hastily introducing a couple of rousing hymns and choruses gave me time to unscramble the chaos at my feet and begin a few minutes later without further interruption.

Another time we were asked to sing from the pulpit, which had steps on either side. We were told that half of us could go on the right side and the other half on the left. I was seated at the electric piano which we had managed to buy some months earlier. The large congregation and I witnessed the chaos which followed. I don't know how many people had fitted into that pulpit before, but fifteen long-skirted women and two guitars squashed in and it was a bit like asking, "How many elephants can you fit into a mini?" Shuffling and squeezing, we took our places; there was certainly not much room to breathe, let alone sing.

However, with a little rearranging, we still managed to lead that particular service.

We still recall the event when we meet up today. "Do you remember, Mag, when your music ended up on the floor or when we were jammed into the pulpit like sardines? Do you remember when your foot went through a rotten floorboard?" Of course, it had to be *my* foot but it was a lucky escape for the piano. Finally, the incident that no one forgot – the night we left Mum behind.

We were frequent visitors to the chapel on the hill where Dad had been a deacon and Mum was still in membership. She always received a wonderful welcome and the company of lots of friends. After the service, we enjoyed the usual refreshments, and then loaded up the cars with instruments, books and Reflectors. All four cars soon pulled up outside my house which happened to be closest and we all piled out for more tea and an extended supper. Mum always went straight to the kitchen during these times to put the kettle on, pour tea and butter sandwiches. It wasn't until none of this happened that one of us said, "Where is Mum?" What a panic! Four of us leapt into the nearest car, sped up the hill to the chapel five minutes away.

Yes! There was Mum standing outside, knowing someone would turn up soon. "So sorry Mum. We all thought that you were with someone else." Long goodbyes had probably caused that, with Mum never leaving the chapel directly and continuing long conversations until well outside on the pavement. We often smiled over that incident and were very glad that we were not further away. Mum was always put into somebody's front seat before any of us moved off again. That became part of the 'Do you remember?' stories and a favourite with Mum, smiling with us all whenever we shared it.

The Reflectors matured in ministry and continued playing for the next twenty years accruing rich experiences.

Vi became a deacon in her Pentecostal fellowship where she still worships and is a very close, special friend right to this day. Maralyn went on to Bible College and trained as a minister and an evangelist. She travels all over the world. She was ordained into the ministry and has recently returned from Florida.

As for me, well I had followed a Bible study year and became involved with the media. However things were about to change and nobody, least of all me, could have begun to imagine what God's plans would be for me.

19

Family News

AUNTIE LILIAN WAS my mother's youngest sister and moved to live near us in the same street in south Wales. As a family, we had always had a dog and Auntie Lil and Uncle Ernie were very fond of ours. One time, a midwifery friend, who was very keen to find a tiny puppy a good home, persuaded us to take a cream coloured poodle named Candy. "Come to supper," she said to the entire group of Reflectors including mother and me of course. Soon, we were all drooling over the last gorgeous bundle of fluff in the litter. I don't know quite how it happened, but Mum and pup were soon together, a tiny face peeping out of Mum's new jacket, snuggling into her chest. Years later Mum said the whole evening had been planned, but it was nothing to do with me of course! Sometime later we saw a photograph taken that evening, with Mum and pup pictured and 'Will she or won't she?' printed underneath. Of course she came home with us a couple of weeks later, beginning a partnership that would last over sixteen years.

We had a dog called Rex before Candy, and he lived through all my comings and goings, well into his fourteenth year. There was a Trixie in our childhood too, and a couple of cats. We also had a budgie for a couple of years, who chatted from morning till night. Peter was my maternal grandmother's bird and came to us after Nan's death in London.

As a result having a family pet we, as a family, took local holidays, usually in a caravan or chalet on the Welsh coastline. After a few years teaching midwifery and living at home with Mum, we bought a small caravan in Porthcawl which accommodated family, friends, Reflectors, dogs and us all for years to come.

Auntie and uncle loved Candy from the first cuddle. "Leave her with us when you go out," they said, which was actually some part of every day. Candy enjoyed two homes from the very beginning, spending long summers and endless holidays on the beach, and in the sea which she loved with both families, for the whole of her life. With equal time spent in both houses, Candy would sit in the window down the road watching the world and his wife go by in the main street of Tonyrefail. The same happened further up the road with us, sometimes in the same day. She also enjoyed walks around the village and rides in the car with both of us of course. Somebody inevitably passed the remark "Gosh, your dog is exactly the same as your auntie's. Are they twins?" I don't think anybody realised that Candy was our dog and equally shared with my uncle and aunt. (Gismo followed Candy which is a whole new story and now we have Blaze who is a young beige coloured whippet.)

The time came for Candy to have her annual check-up with the vet. Mum and I were severely reprimanded because our dog was too fat and the extra weight was not good for her hips and joints. Candy needed a hip replacement for a genetic deformity before she was a year old. We left the vet a little puzzled. As far as we were concerned, our dog's diet was quite ordinary and normal for her breed. One day we called in on auntie unannounced. There was a saucer of full-cream milk, biscuits with tea, a couple of squares of chocolate and a dog showing a distinct fondness for ham sandwiches. "It was auntie," we said during the next visit to the vet. Some treats stayed but most of them had to go.

Auntie was five years younger than Mum and both attended senior citizens and golden hour at the local

Pentecostal church for many years. They both also attended the old age pensioner meetings in the hall at the bottom of our garden. Mum held every position there and retired in her eightieth year, receiving a large engraved wall clock which is keeping perfect time to the present day. They both enjoyed many holidays and activities and had the company and friendship of a great crowd of people.

Auntie called by our house before the meetings started. One particular day we were having a new kitchen built and the workmen were all very busy at the back of the house. The cooker, kettle, washing machine and fridge were all placed one end of the living room. Mum was almost ninety at this time and she always looked forward to seeing her sister dropping in for a cup of tea. I happened to be home that afternoon and as the kettle was boiling I heard the animated conversation behind me falter and change. As Mum and auntie were both Londoners with a distinctive accent, it was impossible for me to know whose speech had altered. I was too terrified to turn around and very afraid of what I would find. In a split second, which seemed an eternity, I turned to see auntie semi-conscious, her head to one side and breathing with difficulty. A few minutes later, an ambulance was at our door. In just a matter of minutes everything had changed. Auntie, as I feared, had suffered a major stroke and died later that same evening. Uncle had died from kidney failure a few years before.

We had no warning as there had been no previous ill health and as far as we knew there were no particular problems. Mum, sitting close to her sister witnessed everything and suffered a deep shock at the speed of her sister's sudden collapse and death. Funeral arrangements had to be made and little did I know then that, in amongst all the sudden grief, my life was turning around once more. I was attending the local Anglican church at this time and the vicar was away. Our curate, who worked in the parish and also at the

Royal Mint said that he would conduct the funeral. "I do that in my time off," he said.

With those few words a switch went on in my head. As I listened to our curate committing auntie to God, I thought in a split-second "I too can do that." I could work as a nurse and work for the church at the same time. That was exactly what I had been doing in Africa and here was the same pattern unfolding before my eyes. I moved easily between hospital midwifery with its multiple tasks, and church with its variety of activities and meetings. I was often present at both, several times in the same day. I had never really seen my chapel or church life bearing any relation to my working life, or co-existing as it had overseas.

So, how were the two going to come together? It could happen; there was no doubt about that. Hadn't I just seen an ordained minister functioning before my eyes, removing his robes and returning to his secular employment? Time would tell how exactly that would happen. The childhood picture with the words 'follow me' were still in my mind and life in Africa and life at home began to merge.

20

Two Jobs

AT AROUND THE same time a very dear friend said, "You should put all your experiences and talents together. Have you thought of ministry in the church? I'll give you a couple of addresses, have a chat to a few people and see what's going on."

A couple of months later it was explained to me how I could be ordained into the Church and remain working as a nurse. I was introduced to the non-stipendiary ministry, at which I was instantly at home.

My personal wish and deep desire to return to Africa had never materialised, as it was influenced by my own unstable health and civil unrest there. Nevertheless, a Christian nurse surrounded by many friends, ministry in the nurses' Christian fellowship and playing the piano with the Reflectors had certainly filled the gap. Stories of my life in the Congo, together with a slide show, were always popular and I was a frequent guest speaker at anniversaries, celebrations and special events. But ordination into the Church was quite a different matter. Here, however was a familiarity, a deep love and a definite coming together. "Do you feel that you have come home?" said the bishop at the time, and I found that I could answer him with confidence: "Yes I have."

It was surprisingly easy fitting into the local church. I had been immersed in Russian Orthodox worship in Belgium. I had often been found in the local Roman Catholic Church and was familiar with liturgy, iconography, vestments, priests and bishops. And also, of course, I was heavily influenced by my friends in the Congo, who cared for me, and kept me safe especially during my lost three days. I had been immersed in silent orders, worship, chants and frequent prayer times. They had all become very familiar as I settled into the Church in Wales.

"I thought I was going to be a nun," I told anyone who would listen. Wise friends said, "Well, you can be an ordained nun. Others have done it, why not you?" I cherished the thought of settling into a family house; it would not have been too far away from home. In my frantic life I longed for the peace and discipline of life in a convent. This was influenced, no doubt, by many friends who belonged to working orders in Cardiff during my own midwifery training days and also those beloved Sisters and priests in the Congo, who held my wellbeing and future in their hands for a few precious years.

Two important meetings were to take place now, both of which could have stopped me in my tracks there and then. The first was a preliminary interview which gave me an introduction to the ordained ministry. I was then invited to a second meeting, held in a vicarage in a rural location. The meeting was scheduled for 6 p.m. However I got off on the wrong foot from the start! I left early for the meeting as I hadn't been on those country lanes before. I'd travelled a couple of miles, then turned a sharp left following the sign to my destination. It seemed that I was quite alone in the world, not even a sheep or cow for company and certainly no farms to be seen. I was on a very narrow track, so narrow that it was impossible to turn around. So there was nothing for it but to press on straight ahead. Another ten minutes and there were a few rooftops in the distance. A couple of miles further on and I hit the top of the village street.

Breathing a sigh of relief, I drew into a small garage to ask for directions to the vicarage.

Before I could say a word, I was greeted by two delighted mechanics. "We have got a three-wheeler in," they said. "Can we put yours on the ramp and check a few things out underneath? Won't be long." My protests about an important appointment went unheard and Robin and I were soon eight feet in the air with the two mechanics underneath. "Who did you say you were going to see?" they said about ten minutes later. "The vicar living just down the road at 6 p.m." I replied. "Well it's past that now. He won't mind, after all you have been helping us out." About fifteen minutes later I rang the vicarage bell. I was greeted with incredulity. "Up on that lonely top road! Up on a ramp in the local garage! Helping them out!" "Yes," I said, "they don't see many three-wheelers around here."

It was an important meeting and not a very promising start for a potential vicar. I thought I was finished before I had begun! Many friends said afterwards that no-one else but my Robin and I would have been up on a ramp when we should have been in the vicarage. Who else indeed!

Over the next few years I questioned the changes taking place in my life and often turned to the four Qs found in one of my textbooks, a book of private devotion written by Pope Clement VI. These words were especially useful when I asked myself the following question. Do I really have to do this?

1 *Volo quidquid vis* – if God wills it; God's presence will be in it.
2 *Volo quia vis* – if God wills it; this becomes the motive.
3 *Volo quomodo vis* – we do it not as we planned; the how is in God's hands.
4 *Volo quamdiu vis* – I must be ready to do this as long as God wills that I should.

21

Parallel Lives

I BEGAN TRAINING for the ministry and joined a whole new crowd of friends: all of us were leading parallel lives in work *and* training for the ministry. We were a very mixed group of solicitors, magistrates, policemen, teachers, social workers, housewives, playgroup leaders, university lecturers, nurses and midwives, a greengrocer and a VAT inspector to mention just a few. We were all launched into the hectic pattern of training for the non-stipendiary ministry, with midwifery and church life being quickly assimilated into it over the next four years.

Meanwhile, the student midwives were on holiday and I was between groups of students. The midwife teacher has to keep her skills up-to-date and so, with much delight, my working life was shared between the labour wards and the community. A wonderful six weeks passed by. I was reconciled to my new direction. Life was vivid and purposeful. The reaction of my colleagues in work was much the same as it had been to the Africa idea many years earlier:

An ordained minister? You laugh too loudly.
Going to Church? At least you will liven things up.
Not finishing work? However will you cope? All the best anyway.

Going out into the community brought back many happy

memories, only this time I was in my own small car and not on a bicycle. There were flats, houses, caravans, bungalows and bedsits to visit. "Where did you say you lived?" became a frequently posed question. Flats gave me a headache right from the start. A good sense of direction was never my strong point. I could have done with a bit of it at that time. Now, you would think that No. 58 was next to No. 59? I did. However that wasn't always the case. I was told: along the green, up the steps, into a different block altogether, along the top, turn left – got it! And when I finished my work and came out I realised that I had lost sight of the car. "I expect it's around the back, nurse, over there," shouted a voice, three floors up.

No. 104, only 50 flats away, can't be that far! Don't you believe it! Eleven floors later, up the stairs with lifts out of order, I was breathless and was found by respective husband propping open his front door. "You should have come up the other side," he said, "only two flights there!" Most of the flats, if not all of them, were perched on the side of a very, very steep hill.

At least houses and flats stayed in one place, but it's another story altogether with caravans. Coming to a stop one day, I found an empty space where the family and the new baby should have been. "You're late nurse. They've moved up there." Peering into the distance I could just about make out a blue speck perched on what looked like the top of a mountain side. I'd have to walk to get there as no car would get me up anywhere near. Clutching my black bag (some things never changed), I set off. It was going to be some climb. Forging ahead into the now pouring rain, I arrived and was soon surrounded by kids and was told that, "They've only just gone out, nurse. We'll tell them you've been." I retreated down the ever increasingly slippery track with the voices now behind me saying, "See you tomorrow." By then I was hoping that I'd be on a day off.

I was leaving another site one particular day and, adjusting my mirror, I drove slowly as I was surrounded by children. I looked hard in the mirror – did I have a passenger? Well, yes I did. Sat up on my back seat, as cheeky as you like, was a little black and tan terrier and in the distance, the owner, who I presumed was chasing after me. "Get out of there," he yelled as he caught up. "Ever so sorry nurse, he gets in everybody's car."

Toddlers can be just as funny. Of course they don't think babies come with the stork anymore, but they are just as interested in everything else that is going on, often stretched out beside Mum and even joining in. Some toddlers cover the babies in kisses just as they're being lowered into the bath; others cover me in kisses, and chocolate sticky ones at that, "'cos you're looking after my baby."

I hadn't spotted any bus drivers this time commentating about my red winter bloomers, as had happened when I was a pupil midwife pedalling my bike. However drivers of other descriptions can be just as cheeky. "Good morning nurse, you won't find a number twenty-one along here." "Shouldn't it be next to twenty?" I innocently asked. "No, it's another block, top of the hill!" I got there, climbed out of my car to furious horn blowing, and found myself jammed between the door of my car and a passing council lorry. "Enjoy the squeeze nurse?" said the friendly voice I'd heard ten minutes earlier! (I think he was the postman. He knew the houses better than I did anyway.)

Often there are no house numbers and no street names and finding the right place on the first attempt takes some doing (especially when you're only filling in for someone else). It was time to revisit the black and cream house: shops in front, bus stop on the right, and park on the left. Good! Everything was in the right place but, something was different about the house. That confused me for a minute, until the husband came to the door. "Please don't change your paint again," I said, "not until I've finished visiting anyway."

It's been great and I've especially enjoyed the little phrases which I still recall today: "Sorry I was slow answering the door nurse; I thought you were from the gas board." "You can't find us?" in response to a call from a phone box, "Don't worry we'll hang the Union Jack out of the window."

Gifts came thick and fast: perfume which was lovely, plenty of cups of tea with lots of cake. No breakfasts were supplied anymore however, as night-time home births became a thing of the past. But one thing never changed, the *welcome* was just the same. The midwife is still a very privileged person, closely joining the family on their very special arrival, an event which remains in the memory forever. "Hello Margaret. It's nice to see you again. Do you remember me?" My mind skidded all over the place trying to place him. Yes, he fitted in somewhere but just where I wasn't sure. "You delivered my son," he said. "He's twenty-three now. I told him I was coming to meet the lady who had brought him into the world."

Still in training for the ministry, I visited the same maternity unit at which I had worked earlier and, having had some parish work nearby, I was still wearing my cassock and cape. "Good heavens! It's you," was the general remark. "We thought it was the Pope, different colour, same design."

I still visit the maternity unit from time to time, and as a result, more lovely people are woven into the fabric of my life. I soak up every minute and am often emotional, dewy-eyed, and sometimes tired. In days gone by, after a hectic shift in the labour ward (with frilly hat slightly askew), I often had reservations about going into the birth book. The photo would be sure to be brought out years later with the comment, "and here's the lady who brought you into the world."

But it was all worth it. A bottle of wine, a bouquet of flowers and lots of thank-you cards. Everybody providing a vital and loving link with the seven-pound bundle tucked up in his or her cot. They were thrilled to bits and so were we the maternity staff.

My first year of ministerial training was soon over. I was now getting used to my new role and quickly finding out that life wasn't any more serious because I was clad from head-to-toe in a black cassock most weekends. I was immersed in a super-duper, hectic sometimes frantic, existence.

*

"She's Penelope," said a charming six-year-old, now an elder sister. "Penelope?" said a sleepy Mum, "Well, well. Penelope she will be." It was the same with Dominic, and his name had to go straight on the birth card. I did wonder what his four-year-old brother would have said if the new baby had turned out to be a girl! But as it happened the name was just right, nobody else had any say in the matter, anyway.

There was a particularly strong family bond amongst the families I dealt with and I was reminded of that when I followed a bridal car up the hill, one day. Now where are they off to, I thought. The maternity unit was the only place straight ahead. I soon found out. We arrived on the postnatal ward. "We've come to see my sister," said the new bride, in all her finery. The whole wedding party was lined up, progressing through the ward with a couple of bridesmaids, pageboys and close relatives. Everybody was thrilled to bits and we all ignored the restricted visitors rule posted on the walls. And what better way for a new baby to meet a large chunk of his extended family. He was soon passed around, admired by everybody – being the centre of attention – although previously of course it had been the bride's special day.

Another time I went into the labour ward where the Mum-to-be was getting along fine and the Dad-to-be was curled up sharing the pillows with her. Quite a lot of the time both of them would drop off to sleep in a warm shaded room, with neither of them disturbed by the midwife popping in and out. Another couple didn't go to sleep but were immersed in watching a TV game show. I said, "I think we'd better go now. The delivery room is free and baby won't be long." "Just a minute sister, another five minutes won't matter will it?" One final contraction came with the end of the programme and so the successful contestant and the brand new Mum and Dad were both pleased.

Occasionally, the baby has had enough and a trip to the nearby operating theatre ends its journey. Dad follows sometimes and watches delivery. Most times he's in the nursery chewing his nails. Baby's arrival comes in a matter of minutes, usually a pink, screaming 7lb bundle ready to give to Dad. "Me! Hold him, I'll drop him!" He doesn't of course, and is soon totally immersed in counting fingers and toes.

Gone were the days when we had to bike around Cardiff. Gone too was the time we spent trying to find Dad-to-be, usually in the local watering hole. Now, all these years later the ward phone rings nonstop – everybody wants to know what's going on, and father-to-be doesn't leave the labour ward until baby has arrived. Some come well prepared though. One, arriving late in the afternoon from work, soon made himself at home. "I'll make you a cup of tea," I said. "Oh it's all right," he replied, "I've brought some with me." Out came a flask of tea, followed by sausage rolls, sandwiches, chocolate biscuits, and a lump of fruit cake thrown in for good measure. "I won't go hungry will I?" he said with a grin on his face. That wasn't the end of it. Around midnight the outside bell rang and mother-in-law had arrived with fresh supplies. "Got to keep his energy up Sister. He's been at work all day!" That particular father was very comfortable with us and was eventually joined by the entire close family, on both sides, when baby was born around seven the next morning.

*

Most of my training for the ministry ran alongside midwifery teaching without any major problems. However as I went into the third year and dissertations with tight deadlines spilled over into the holidays, I began to have serious doubts that my two lives were going to flow quite so easily once I was ordained.

I reached a decision just as I passed my fiftieth birthday. I just could not continue with long journeys to the hospital, irregular shifts and the unpredictability of finding myself still in the labour wards when I was expected to take a service, funeral or wedding. It would have been so much easier and so much more straightforward if I was not in the self-supporting ministry. Both church and hospital were expecting 100 per cent commitment from me. Having been a salaried worker for half of my working life, the prospect of early retirement was met with much dismay. Advice was freely given: "You have a good ten years yet." "Don't be foolish." "Give this some very serious thought." I did and with much prayer, mostly given whilst on foot dashing between both areas; there really was no alternative.

I didn't have enough savings to finish work completely and was offered a few alternatives in the National Health Service, but life would have been just as hectic. Then my mind jumped right back to my time nursing the elderly in Belgium and I had a flash of inspiration. Why couldn't I do that again? Life with the elderly and infirm would be at a much slower pace and I could work nearer to home, almost in the parish. The fact that I halved my pension and salary in one fell swoop caused some of my mentors some concern, but I certainly was not the first and neither would I be the last to survive on the reduced income. I was living at home with Mum which was very good for both of us. And of course there was a lot of sense now in driving a Reliant Robin which was exceptionally economical and fitted my new financial status perfectly.

I left the maternity unit after a surprise party in the middle of the night. Looking at the photos now we all looked drunk but of course we were not. Shaded lights and the time of night made us look tired, not tipsy. Late morning saw me leaving them all behind clutching the photo of the last baby I brought into the world to keep with the photo of the first baby that I had delivered thirty years earlier. I was now to be launched on a new dual career path that would sustain me for the next ten years.

At this time I wasn't too far from my ordination and the midwifery and nursing staff wanted to support me and join in the celebration. The self-supporting ministry was my choice because I had accepted it as being God's choice. After selection and going through training and placement in several parishes, I began to realise that life and work at home was not going to be much different from what it had been overseas.

The concept of this ministry is based on the apostle Paul's example when he insisted that he would earn his own living, and would not be a burden to his Christian converts. Roland Allan, a pioneer in the development of this kind of ministry, had spent many years working in East Africa. He called for a return to biblical principles following the example of the apostle Paul. Over the years, Roland Allan's idea began to bear fruit and since 1970 this ministry has grown rapidly, sometimes called the supplementary or self-supporting ministry. The more I read and learned, the more my African preparation and work came to the fore. I was soon very much at home working in the parish and nursing the elderly just as I had been doing with the mission and midwifery in Africa, moving easily between the two. I did find the lengthy training thorough and demanding but it all fell into place when I was out working in the parish and hospital, exactly as I had before.

Sometimes I began my working day in my nurse's uniform, changing into cassock and collar a few hours later. I moved between services and wards through the 24-hour clock. I had periods of rest and a day or so off now and again (something which had never happened in Africa!). I worked through the night and celebrated the Eucharist; I conducted evensong and nursed all through the night. In Africa I used to be called to services with the beating of the drum; now I was called with the pealing of church bells.

I conducted weddings and funerals, changed uniform, and then returned to nursing work at home. In Africa I exchanged my white nurse's dress for six yards of brightly coloured cloth and a pretty top whenever I visited a women's group, choir practice or Bible study. Here at home I soon settled into my round-the-clock existence with groups of different people. Easter, Christmas, Mothering Sunday, Christingle, Communion were all wonderful experiences with family friends and parish. Patients got used to me completing a medicine round in my role as a nurse, and then seeing me disappear for a few minutes only to reappear as the minister.

Colleagues came to the funerals which I conducted, as we'd cared for the same people together. Weddings were great fun of course with me dressed in my very best, as colleagues were married and later babies were born. I never missed the christenings either.

Nursing colleagues came from many different areas, but

I never had my own church. I was always deeply grateful to my friends and ministers who loaned me their buildings, often joining in with me, where work and parish blended evenly into one.

Before all that happened of course I had to complete my training and endless assessments. We were all sent away for a final retreat before ordination. At our last breakfast together we all gathered in collars and best clothes. I looked in a full-length mirror gazing at the very mature woman in a cornflower blue dress and a very unfamiliar collar. I wistfully let my mind wander back to my early youth when I was draped in six yards of multicoloured cloth and flip flops, burned yellow under the African sun, so sure I would be there for the rest of my life. Now I was beginning a new phase, confident that this step was God's choice and whereas before I walked the jungle paths, I now walked the city streets and found that God was exactly the same – no different from the yesterday that had gone, just the same in the present, on this very special day, and would be the same forever into the future.

At our ordination, we all entered the cathedral, smiling at family and friends. We were robed in brand new albs, carrying our white stoles over our right arm. Soon we would be ordained and leave the cathedral as reverends. It seemed such a huge step to all of us. For me it was unbelievable and, as I took my seat, I said to myself: "Only God could have done this."

As I waited for my turn to be photographed with the bishop, I caught a glimpse of so many colleagues from my old life in midwifery and my new life in nursing the elderly. The bishop asked, "Who were all those people waving, Margaret, as you came up to the altar?" They were all behind the high altar in the Lady Chapel. "Oh, they are all midwives and nurses, Father. We all work together." "Well," said the bishop, "I think that is just wonderful." As we grouped for a photograph, with a very unfamiliar robe and a deacon's sash around me, I thought it was all absolutely wonderful too!

Mum was in her mid-eighties on this lovely day and, as I stood by the bishop for the customary photograph, he said, "Call your mother over Margaret." That was such a special moment. Mum who had walked every step of the way from my pre-nursing days, now stood with me after my ordination. I often look at that photograph now and cherish the moment when a very special Mum was invited to join me on a very special day.

As time passed I found my mirror image. Here was the active and powerful mission which I had viewed with African eyes. Now I found nothing had changed. God's mission and ministry to His people was a continuous chain of unbroken links all over His world, and here I was once again joining so many others, right in the middle of it all. This was the familiar ministry which paid no wages, and just provided me with sufficient – no different from my early preparation and life. I was on home ground now and didn't have to use two languages to work and minister. Here was God's promise fulfilled:

You can be a missionary for me wherever you are.

Here was my beloved Dad's wish fulfilled:

Carry on with your missionary work.

I can say now with absolute certainty that the non-stipendiary ministry has allowed me to do just that.

I wasn't that young anymore and I was often tired but there were lots of bonuses: life at home, being with Mum, and Dave now married with a family of his own.

My multicultural life had expanded. I worked for and with many others of differing faiths. I often looked up to find friends of other faiths listening to the words of Jesus in the Eucharist, the Lord's Prayer and Gospel readings. There was never any antagonism.

"I always feel safe when you're on duty," the staff sometimes told me. "God is with you, so we will all be safe," they added. Night duty, experiencing death for the first time, brought fear to some members of staff. Later, sharing a cup of tea, most would say, "Glad you were here with us tonight." Life went on and both parish and nursing homes brought a whole new wealth of experiences. Many said that I'd never get used to not being a midwife, as I'd always had babies around me. But, babies didn't disappear from my life altogether either. I've been on more than one hair-raising bus, car or coach trip with a heavily pregnant parishioner. They'd say: "I can stay now or go to that party, concert or event; no need to worry, now that you're here." After all, they say that a midwife and minister are all wrapped up in the same package.

One time, the curate in our home parish rang and said: "My wife is very upset as our midwife is out on call. Can you come?" I arrived to find a teary mum-to-be clutching her tummy. Gulping her breath she told me that baby hadn't moved for hours and that something must be wrong. "Oh he's gone to sleep, I expect," I said recalling thirty-odd years of experience, "after all there's no night or day in the womb is there?" Separated from the tools of my trade and my uniform I hoped I sounded confident, "Would you like me to wake him up?" I offered. I pointed out the firm line of the baby's back and the knobbly hands and feet. Gently moving one towards the other, I said "Wake up now, you're worrying your Mum and Dad." He stretched (they do you know), and kicked out in protest, then continued to thump his delighted Mum from inside for the rest of the evening. "Very useful having you about," was their parting comment. "Don't tell your midwife," I said, "she may decide to preach my sermon on Sunday!"

This tale must have got round however, for another pregnant friend wanted to identify the hands and feet of her baby, to convince herself that there was a real little person inside. "I wish you hadn't done that," said her husband some time later, "she's totally absorbed now and chats to her tummy most of the time." Can't win them all!

Sometimes time itself was a bit tight, and I often found that I had to leave the parish to go to the nursing home without changing from one uniform into another. (I've since learned that it's much easier to wear the both together!) The first time I turned up in my cassock at the nursing home, I was greeted with cries of dismay. "We hope you haven't come to bury us," they wailed! My status went up no end though and, apart from the coloured blouse and small heel on the shoe, I looked exactly like the chaplain I was told... or... you look the same as him Mag! They soon got to know me however and became quite used to me changing on the spot.

"Gosh, how do you manage all these buttons Mag? I'll help." The skirt was straightened, buttons fastened or unfastened by a nurse on her knees. "Oh you look different now Mag," on leaving for ministry work. "We'll have to call you something else." Mag will do, I told them as I was still the same person underneath.

The boot was sometimes on the other foot. A number of parishioners took great interest in their curate working as a nurse and turned up to see me in action. So, off went the cassock and on went the blue nurse's dress or what the gardener described as a 'snazzy outfit'. Giving out medicines, helping with meals, nursing the sick, getting on with the job was quite a novelty to some at first, and gradually they got used to my two different roles.

The biggest change came on a Sunday morning following the service. Shaking hands with the *vicar*, the conversation would go something like this: "Yes, the baby's lovely, just like his father or grandma. He/she is good really… no trouble at all." Then the family group would reach the *curate* (me) and the conversation would change to labour pains, spots, wind, nappy rash, baby weight, lack of sleep and sticky eyes. All on the church steps!

It went right across the board really. "I should have gone to see the nurse today but you're here now. What do you think of this weight, diet, blood pressure etc.?" as I joined in at the morning coffee group. Women's problems were whispered in a huddle. The vicar was warned off with the words "go away" when he tried to join in a group. "This is women's talk."

There was bound to be an overlap I suppose. I'm really at home conducting christenings. I don't handle the babies as if they're made of china, or as if I'm holding a rugby ball. And of course there's the added bonus of christening parties and I never say no to them. What I love these days is that I'm still around as the babies grow and to a midwife, that is a bonus. Maternity care in the hospital ends at ten days and very often much before that. Now I get to see them smile at me over the communion rail, with chubby hands reaching for a full chalice.

Some children shriek noisily through my sermons. (I do try to tell parents not to leave and that I won't be long but many don't believe that!) Some children chuck and hurtle their toys all over the place, then get on their feet and run into the kid's corner. For them, Sunday school comes fast on its tail. On one occasion I received a cutting of a cartoon taken from a national newspaper, when lady vicars first came on the scene. That provoked comments from all over the place. The picture showed a lady vicar conducting a service when, judging by the look on the other lady's face, she was well into labour. Leaning over her the lady vicar said: "It's just lucky for you dear that I happen to be a midwife as well!" Me to a T of course! That caused so much fun that a friend in the church enlarged, copied, painted and framed it and then presented it to me. It's nice to know I suppose that my other skills will always be there if any such emergency cropped up... and needless to say the vicar did look remarkably like me.

I'm often asked by colleagues and friends about my clothes. Most of my parish work is done in a cassock, which is a long black garment covering me completely from head to foot. It's hard wearing, serviceable but very hot in summer. "You could wear a swimsuit under that and nobody would know," was the advice given to me, as I visibly wilted in the hot weather. But, that's not quite right either, as swimsuit wasn't the first suggestion, it was bikini! I'd be wary of either garment anyway, just in case I should faint and most of me would be revealed. I'll stick to a skirt and blouse whatever the temperature. I'm wonderfully warm in winter though, and nobody is likely to find out what's underneath.

The first cassock I wore in training was a garment designed for a man: totally shapeless with thirty-nine tiny buttons right down the front from neck to hemline and all on the wrong side – try doing them up in a hurry! (Thirty-nine buttons signify the sources of Anglican belief.) This garment had slits on the sides but I didn't take much notice of those until I asked the question, "Where does a lady keep her handkerchief when wearing a cassock?" The slits were only designed to reach trouser pockets. I just hoped I wouldn't have a cold. A handbag somehow doesn't seem right to carry in just before the start of a service.

This cassock reached the edge of my shoes, or at least I thought it did, until one of the congregation told me that my ankles were too thin for black stockings. I like black stockings. I like black lace seamed stockings or tights, a lot depended on which ones I picked up first. I've got a drawer full: yellow, green, red, blue, purple, any colour would have done, so I wasn't too bothered about black.

So the cassock didn't hide the colour of the tights which clad my legs, but even if it was a little short it didn't stop the vicar behind treading on it. "Get off my cassock," was a common request as we approached the chancel steps. This always produced a grin from the congregation, but had little effect on him, it seems. He said he wasn't used to having a woman in front of him and I certainly wasn't used to having a vicar behind me, not then anyway.

Later on, with another vicar, I was told "Your black lace stockings make me throw up," as he shoved two fingers down his throat to hammer home the point. "Your cassock's too short, get another one." Well! I was close to getting a new one anyway but I wasn't ready to part with my tights. "Part of my economy drive," I told him, "as they don't snag or ladder." But, as the weather got warmer they had to go, of course.

Another time I treated myself to a pair of multicoloured, but predominantly turquoise, balloon-shaped trousers. I thought they were quite the thing and they were comfortable under my cassock. One day, I was standing in front of the congregation and happened to look down at my feet and was horrified to see a good couple of inches of multicoloured trousers beneath my cassock. Nobody said anything... certainly not by the person in charge of me at the time then, or perhaps he had his head in his hands and his eyes shut tight!

People must have taken notice though, because when that newspaper cartoon was painted, there were multicoloured trousers painted in beneath my cassock. And just to rub it in, it was painted in exactly the same colours as the stained glass window behind the vicar, who looked startlingly like me of course.

This particular parish staffed a community shop in the High Street, and lots of my clothes came from there, with most of them chosen by somebody else. "That'll suit

Margaret. We thought of you when we saw that." I had a whole cupboard-full of multicoloured mohair jumpers and very warm they were too. However a request was eventually left in the shop: "Don't sell her anything furry ever again." The vicar probably had an allergy to mohair, but I liked them and they were very warm.

Soon afterwards however, I turned up to find a jacket waiting for me which knocked mohair jumpers off their pedestal. This thick woollen-lined jacket has been dubbed Joseph's multicoloured dream coat. When I turned up to work in that, all the nurses wanted one. It was bright purple with overprints of every vivid colour imaginable. If multicoloured mohair was too much to handle, then this item was certainly over the top! I don't remember any special remarks from anybody, but lots of people covered their eyes and I expect the vicar did as well.

In time I was duly measured for my new cassock. "For goodness sake, measure her properly," was the instruction to the shop. That was done and I was covered in 53 inches of black cloth instead of the earlier 50 inches and it was quite different from the other one.

Many people were now waking up to the fact that there was an ever-growing number of women about to be ordained and it eventually filtered through to the ministerial outfitters. Cassocks were styled with us in mind: same colour of course, same thirty-nine buttons but all on the right side this time, with darts in the right places, a waistline, and three deep pleats in the back. "Give us a twirl," was often mentioned in the parish and nursing home and of course I obliged. I then went overboard and finished it off with a short, black shoulder cape. No slits in this one; just deep pockets and in went car keys, notes, handkerchief and anything else to hand, with it being filled up regularly with what I call my cassock sweets.

On the whole this cassock had some extras and was a

definite improvement. But, as I was soon to find out, some disadvantages would trip me up. I was called to visit a hospital only to find the lifts had broken down. With four floors of stairs to negotiate, I soon found out that it was impossible to climb four flights of stairs in a longer cassock. Nevertheless, I stepped forth and passed a lot of smiling faces on the way up and on the way down.

My red face on both accounts provoked the remark from a passing nurse that perhaps going down would be easier if I slid backwards down the banisters. Tempted as I was, I don't think nurse or minister would have got away with that one.

On leaving a church which was on the side of a very steep hill, I faced countless steps leading down to the pavement. Turning slightly to the person behind me I nearly hurtled from top to bottom and just avoided breaking my neck. That happened because of the extra three inches – ideal for standing still or walking in a straight line but, steps and stairs are definitely out.

I worked as a deacon in my first parish for three and a half years whilst also working in the nursing home. Then the Anglican Church took a vote and overturned years of religious history and tradition. Women could be ordained as priests and I was on the list for ordination into the priesthood the following June. Yes!

22

Surprises in the Family

WE HAVE HAD many surprises in our family, most of them very unexpected. Mum had long given up on me, as far as a wedding, husband and a family were concerned. Her expectations ended around about the time I was thirty. With years of travelling and study behind me, her hopes of extending the family through me were gone for good.

Those expectations were not extended to David who was also enjoying his singleton status. By now he was a Baptist minister and, with our busy lives, Mum happily joined us both in the flurry of activities and was never short of friends and days out.

Imagine our total surprise then when one day David announced that he had met his future wife and they would be married in the near future. Our delight knew no bounds when a year or so later we anticipated the birth of a baby into our family, turning Mum into Nan and me into a doting auntie.

We cuddled and most definitely spoilt a very handsome healthy bundle that quickly turned our lives upside down. David-John turned into a dimple-cheeked chubby toddler, and was all too soon attending a Welsh primary school at four years of age. Mum and I wondered where the baby time had flown by when we looked at the first school photo, showing a very independent boy in school uniform and tie, gazing back at us.

As the years passed David-John was ready to go to

secondary school. At the same time, David's marriage failed and he returned home to live with Mum and me. Dad had never lived in this house and so, a two-up two-down with a small kitchen had been big enough for me and Mum. David however became very unwell, needing several hospitalisations over several years. When he was better, he returned to my room while I used the settee. This could not be a long term solution, so the builders arrived and David moved into a large-sized loft, with plenty of room for David-John when he came to stay.

At this time I was following another training course and David-John was about to sit his GCSEs. My nursing colleagues also had children sitting the same exams and they asked me how many exams I thought DJ (we'd shortened his name a few years earlier) would pass. "Well, he doesn't say much about the subjects he's studying – he's very laid back like his Dad. We don't really know. His schoolwork is OK so we are hoping for the best," I told them. As a doting aunt, I decided to drive a bargain with my nephew. "DJ," I said, "I'll promise you £50 for every exam you pass, OK?" expecting to stimulate him to achieve five at the most. "OK auntie, deal done."

Sometime later my laid-back nephew passed eight exams with two resits leaving me £500 worse off. I was left to fill the black hole resulting from his unexpected, but very pleasant success. Needless to say I stayed quiet when his A levels came around. Success still followed, however, with DJ going to University College of Wales, Cardiff, which delighted David no end. And, in between the two sets of exams, a few more surprises would be in store.

A few years earlier, David had been asked by DJ to go to west Wales (where he was living at the time), as he had some news for him. DJ had met his first girlfriend and over that weekend introduced her to his Dad. That same year Maria joined us for a week during our summer holiday and celebrated her sixteenth birthday with us, with DJ having just turned sixteen in March of the same year. The next two years were very busy with frequent visits from DJ and Maria. Sport and leisure had become DJ's main interest and he began to study and prepare for employment in the leisure industry. His Freshers' week at university coincided with the birth of our lovely Caitlin, turning David into Grandad and Mum into great Nan and me into a doting great Aunt. The loft conversion for David was joined by an extension to the back of our little house where Maria and Caitlin lived while DJ was at university.

So, here I was, with a baby in the family again and one under our roof this time. My delight was overwhelming, only being slightly less than Mum's deep joy as she cuddled her great-granddaughter morning, noon and night. Maria and DJ, together with Caitlin, moved into their own house when DJ was able to live out at university. When they were packed up and ready to go, our tears flowed freely as we waved them off. But they quickly returned at the weekend, just a few days later.

Their visits were very regular and so were our visits to them. Mum, who had by now entered her nineties, was in her element. We pushed our beautiful baby around Tonyrefail in the pram, and pushed her on the swings in the park. Grandad took us all on frequent trips out and a wonderful time was had by us all.

Our beautiful Courtney, fair like her mother as Caitlin was as dark as her father, arrived amidst great love; she was a gorgeous nine-pound bouncer. Sadly Mum did not live to see Courtney, but she would have loved and cuddled her morning, noon and night, just as she did with Caitlin.

David-John, like his father before him, was sadly to find out that relationships can come to an end and Maria, four-year-old Caitlin and Courtney stayed in Cardiff while he returned home once more to west Wales.

I have lovely pictures coming to mind as I remember David's surprised face when toddler Caitlin shouted out 'Grandad' for the first time. His face was wreathed in smiles when he was acknowledged as Grandad for the second time around too.

Time passed by and DJ met Aleshya and Maria met Steve. "This is the man I want to marry," Maria told me over coffee one day. That day did come, and I married them which was a happy day for all of us and launched us into a whole new experience with an ever-expanding family. Steve's three children from a previous marriage soon blended in with our two and every other weekend all of us just about fitted around the family-sized table for dinner. Who would have thought that we would be nine for Sunday lunch, with two dogs looking on too! How Mum would have loved all that.

By now, Caitlin is eight years of age and Courtney three years old. Dave and I are surrounded by children; our house is like a railway station, as they all come and go from different ends of the country. Their dog Buster and or dog Blaze fortunately get on, and they are often found curled up together head to tail. They curl up together at night time too but this time at the foot of my bed, which leaves very little room for me!

At a very early age Caitlin developed an interest in ponies and horses and as a four-year-old she was confident enough to ride a large pony at the local riding school. She has continued to have lessons ever since and four years down the line she is still very involved with the stables and turning into a good little rider. Mucking out at the stables is the highlight of her day and nothing as yet has altered her devotion to ponies. Courtney, on the other hand, is quite different, keeping her distance from the stables and showing no desire to follow her sister. Dancing is her first love and she began lessons as soon as she was three.

Sometimes I think of our families. First, Dave and I,

secure and loved in the home Mum and Dad made for us. Then I think of Dave and Mary raising their son DJ in their family. Then, all too soon, DJ was establishing his own family with Maria. Now it is Steve and Maria nurturing their family of five with a safe home for them all. We also have close family living in Porthcawl with our aunt Rosabelle, shortened to aunty Betty, our father's only surviving sibling. Our cousins and their families are rapidly expanding. Others live outside Wales in Somerset, Herne Bay and London.

Then I think of Jacob's dream in the book of Genesis, where he settled for the night using stones as pillows to lay down to sleep. Jacob had a dream that a ladder was set up on earth with the top of it reaching heaven and the angels of God ascending and descending it. God spoke to Jacob and said, "The land you lie on will be yours. Your seed will spread to all corners of the earth and in your seed all the families of the earth will be blessed." I like to think that all families everywhere began just there; your family and mine, blessed by God through each generation.

23

Robin

A LIFE SPENT constantly on the move and always amongst crowds of people has left me, as some would describe, on my own. Some people chat to me on the street or whilst shopping, "You have had a wonderful life," they say "but is there anything you would like to change?" Meaning in a nice way, wouldn't you like to have been married?

My marriage stakes after all were never very high, because I disappeared from home at regular intervals: to Blaugies, Brussels, Birmingham, Antwerp and a long stretch in Africa; they were hardly conducive to settling down. A great interest was taken in any budding friendship and, on winning a very pretty vase in a church jumble sale, I was told to put it away in my bottom drawer. Giving a lift in the car to any man caused a great interest, and so brought doom on any possible friendship from the start. Once I thought I'd play a trick on all the matchmakers.

Talking to a large group of people I began like this: "As you all know, I have led a very busy life, but today I am going to fill in some of the missing pieces. My life has taken on a whole new dimension. It has become even more unpredictable, exciting and great fun. Today I am going to tell you about Robin, my Robin, partner and friend. Over twenty years ago I formed a very close relationship which has grown even closer over the years. (A closet affair!) I was introduced to Robin and it was love at first sight." Now there was a gleam in their eyes; I had their undivided attention.

"I soon became inseparable from my new-found friend and couldn't do without him at all (things were certainly hotting up now). I could never bear to part with him (that's more like it) and I can say very definitely that we will never be separated (sure to be a wedding at last!). Robin and I will always be together: my faithful, bright yellow three-wheeler friend."

Was there a sigh? Certainly a giggle. After all, I'd walked and wobbled on a bike all over the place. In the past, I'd trusted my life to strangers all over the world on trains, boats and planes. But now I was independent – I was sitting in my own little car driving all over the place and soon we would be sharing all sorts of experiences together.

Robin took on his own personality and friends; people didn't ask "How is your car these days?" Rather, they said "Is Robin all right?" or "Robin not well, gone to the garage for a few days? Hope he will soon be better," and so on. He was never unwell for long, just an annual check up, a service or MOT. "Oh, Robin is back," everybody would say when he returned, shiny and ready for more journeys. "It must be like sitting in a bowl of custard," was a general remark passed on to me when viewing my bright yellow car. It was called the 'bananamobile' in work and nurses piled into it to go home and it likewise caused hysterical laughter in the parish.

One day I lost matron when she was supposed to be following me. "You drive too fast," she said and, having being seen hurtling around a corner with only one wheel at the front, Robin was renamed the Yellow Peril. I thought I'd heard it called all names under the sun, but when a passing parishioner saw me driving in a different direction, she said "Now where is that Yellow Canary going?" I don't always speed, in fact I don't speed at all; but a very windy night can add a few miles on to the speedometer. Once, whilst walking to the car on a very blustery night with several parishioners,

I was helped along by a rousing chorus of "Yellow bird, up high in banana tree."

The street alongside the church where I was working at the time was very narrow and having filled the car with parishioners, it took a nine-point turn to face the right way home. Hysterical giggles filled the car and the following comment caused us a great deal of fun: "Why bother to watch *The Vicar of Dibley* when we have our own version right here?" That reminded me of a conversation in the nursing home: "There would be more people in church if they were more like the vicar of Dibley." "Seen Mag lately," followed that. "She is better than that."

We went all over the place and I didn't have to sign an attendance sheet or introduce myself as my yellow car had been seen first, taking its place amongst the more sombre black, grey and blue clerical cars. "Why don't you change that car, we worry about you?" But I wasn't keen to do that. After all, Robin could turn round on a ten pence piece, and I was away before the larger models had got moving.

Sadly my yellow car eventually had to go – the paint outliving the engine. However it was soon replaced by the brightest scarlet red anybody had ever seen. Robin and I are just as friendly and always jammed with people wherever we go. "Can you give us a lift Mag?" said three colleagues who had just finished the night shift with me. "Of course, get in." I did, they did, and we were watched by the entire day staff and matron through the conservatory window. Later that night, a note was left by matron: 'If anybody wants a ride in Margaret's car I'm taking bookings now!'

Yes, Robin and I caused quite a stir. Many people seem to think that we can't do the things we do: like reversing, three-point turns, getting around at a reasonable speed with room for three and me.

Once, on the way to work, something happened that nearly finished Robin and me off for good. Many of the nursing homes in the Rhondda are surrounded by narrow country lanes with very little room for vehicles to pass each other. I rounded a bend to find a very large stationary transporter lorry in front of me. Unable to stop in time, Robin and I went right underneath it. Somewhere above me, the driver shouted "Don't try to get out whatever you do! I'll try to reverse off the roof. Sound the horn if you are worried." I most certainly was. I had visions of bits of me and bits of fibreglass, both bright red, all messed up together. "No good," said the same voice, "I'll have to phone the fire brigade to take the roof off and lift you out." Poor Robin, poor me! I managed to wriggle across to the other side (just as well I'm small), open the door and push it into the hedge and slide out into several inches of muddy icy water. "Well done," said the driver. "I'll squeeze into the hedges and you can try to drive out as I reverse off your roof." He did it that time and I sped away, very thankful that Robin and I were still in one piece.

When I arrived at work some time later, I was ready to tell the tale, in a very welcome coffee break. "We don't believe you," said my colleagues. They didn't until I took them out at the end of the shift to see the tyre marks clearly visible on the roof.

From that time onwards Robin was called the 'corned beef tin' and it took years to live that one down.

One of my wardens once said, "I'm worried about you." "Why is that?" I asked. "Well, I saw you go up that steep hill in your car, and if you can go uphill as fast as that it worries me at what speed you will come down." Another time I looked in my rear view mirror and one of my nurses and his girlfriend were clinging on to each other in the back and were decidedly white around the gills. "Are you all right?" I asked. "Goes pretty fast your car doesn't it" was their reply!

Some still express surprise when they find out about my car. Once, I had to phone a vicar up to explain that I would be a little late arriving. "What did you say you drive, a three-wheeler – a reverend in a three-wheeler car?" Surprise is such that sometimes I deliberately conceal it when conducting a wedding or a funeral and pick it up later a few streets away. I haven't seen many reverends, if any, getting around the way I do and I would be interested to know if I have any fellow vicars who own three-wheelers. I don't think that there are many of us about.

Of course, I don't ever speed. I can't with a little car and a small engine but I must admit, I have great enthusiasm for moving reasonably fast and overtaking much bigger, more powerful vehicles than mine. Yes, I suppose I look fast and, as I said, a good tail wind adds on another 10 m.p.h. without any trouble at all.

Many concerned people advised me to get rid of the car. "After all you could afford a four-wheeler now can't you? Think of your Mother, four doors would be helpful and wouldn't she be more comfortable?" Mum loved her very frequent trips out with Robin and me. Anyway, she was able to be comfortable in David's up-to-date model, which was more spacious, steadier and had four doors as well.

However there is one very good reason why Robin and I will never be parted. Robin Reliant cars, because of their lightweight bodies, are technically classed as a motorbike requiring only a B1 license (old category group C). I passed my driving test for a motorbike license but I couldn't drive a car with four wheels as I hadn't passed that particular driving test. Over the years I have thought about changing Robin for what some would call a sturdier car. There was one occasion when I decided to grasp the challenge, and so I paid for a series of driving lessons and chose the sportiest little red four-wheeler model in a local showroom window.

"No problem Margaret," said my instructor. "You will sail through." The day finally arrived and the test was completed in the driving school car. I drove as I usually did. I had been mobile for some years by now. But the expression on the face of the examiner as he clumped his board on his knee told me the worst. I had failed. I went straight back into Robin, drove to the showroom and watched the sold notice on the new four-wheeler car being taken off. Acute disappointment washed over me.

Several further tests followed. The last one, a couple of years ago, finished me altogether. The reason being, amongst other things I suppose, was that I had come too close to shaving the elephant. My mind boggles, especially after being in the Congo. Apparently I had come too close to stationary traffic I was told. Nevertheless Robin and I were straightaway off on our own again.

By this time we had been together for twenty years. We had skidded and slid all over the place. Fog, torrential rain and thunderstorms had not deterred us, and we had never turned over or landed upside down in a ditch, which was the concern of most people at the time. Robin has never let me down – he is now a more sombre wine red. Now I don't give into pressure and Robin and I are still trundling along. At this moment, while I am still driving, I can confidently say that Robin and I will never be parted – never!

24

Nursing Home Animals

"It would be good to have a pet for the residents," announced matron in a staff meeting one day. Most of us thought a budgie, or a couple of canaries or even an aquarium with soothing fish would be good. "I'm not sure," she responded, "it's going to be extra work to clean out a cage or a fish tank." The doctor suggested a dog, a nice friendly placid Labrador that would be good company for the residents. If a bird in a cage or fish in a tank would cause extra work, then feeding and walking a dog would be out of the question too, surely?

How about a cat? We seemed to have reached a compromise, ruling out fish, birds and a dog, for the foreseeable future anyway. We were thinking of a fully-grown, well-behaved cat from the local rescue centre. What we got were six-week-old twin tabby kittens. When they arrived they eyed us all with disgust, as if they'd arrived in the worst possible place, but they soon made themselves feel at home.

Several squeaking toys, titbits and porridge for breakfast, convinced them that being with us would not be so bad after all. They soon realised that there were some advantages in living in a community of nearly fifty people. They quickly learned how to twist us all around their little paws and we named them Topsy and Turvy and they soon lived up to those names.

Those two tiny bundles of fur took over, and everybody

watched their antics with amazement. They vaulted over the backs of twenty chairs. They scampered up four pairs of long, blue velvet curtains. They hurtled along thirty feet of multicoloured carpet, generally keeping everybody alert and amused. Their antics were a definite change from the usual television or radio programmes constantly blaring on in the background.

Some escapades could not be allowed however, such as the sharpening of claws on elderly laps, furniture and newly painted walls and varnished doors. So we brought in a cat scratching post with a revolving mouse at the top and they happily clawed their way around that. They had beds with their names on, but the carpeted stairs or warm laundry baskets were much better. And of course, a cosy lap, of which there were many to choose from, as they got bigger, was absolute bliss.

We all entered the world of vaccinations and spaying. Frequent daily cries of "Shut that door," and the risk of one or both exploring the grounds in their early months, gave us visions of being overrun with kittens a few years down the line. Flea collars, worm medicine and visits to the vet became part of the work routine and part of life in the residential nursing home.

They were quickly registered as Topsy and Turvy and fitted comfortably into one cat transporter until they got bigger and started shoving each other around, leaving us no option but to buy another one and give them a bit more space. Ten pence on the coffee money usually covered most needs and they were often on the receiving end of lots of gifts from friends and families who were delighted with the addition of the two lively kittens who had brightened up the day for residents and families.

I was charged with taking them to the vet some distance away. On the first visit, the vet asked, "Which one is which?" I stared at him blankly but a name wrapped around each collar solved that one. A more observant colleague noticed a heavy black streak down Turvy's back, or was it Topsy? The risk of overdosing one and ignoring the other was high.

After a simple operation the kittens were neutered and the vet advised us to make sure the night nurses kept an eye on them and not to let them chew their stitches. He also said that they were too fat. No more porridge for them and no pay rise for the staff that cared for them so well on the night shift.

Both cats, by now almost a year old, soon recovered. Work was never going to be the same again. Many a phone call was rudely interrupted by an inquisitive paw. Was that Topsy or Turvy? Which one was it this time was the query when the caller rang back after the guilty cat had been dispatched to her bed under the desk? They found their way back of course, pencils and pens flying to the floor. Books and papers were sat on and the food and biscuits dropped on the floor became a welcome present. They often wrapped themselves around any available neck, refusing to budge for anybody, making themselves at home, which was observed by all our visitors.

Nursing homes receive a large variety of visitors, and inspections are made from time to time. One group of inspectors was most impressed when they observed the residents' smiling faces and, looking at the cats' food, beds and toys, the remark was passed on that the cats were so well looked after, the care of the residents as a result must be even better, *par excellence*, second to none. So Topsy and Turvy remained as worthy members of the household, proving their worth and were rewarded with sardines for supper, which was one of their favourites.

One particular day that I shall never forget began with a phone call asking if we would like to enrol in a 'pets as therapy' scheme. The following week, three dogs came to visit, chosen for their suitable size, friendliness and adaptability.

During this first visit Topsy was found spitting from a great height on the top of the cupboard, and the quieter Turvy hid under a long flowing tablecloth. If anything got too much for her she would disappear for hours; she was sometimes discovered under a bed upstairs. She wasn't at all like her bossy sister, Topsy, who would stay around to brazen things out. (Now, after many visits, all the animals stare each other out and keep to opposite ends of the room.)

When I was on a day off, I sometimes turned up with Mum and our dog Gismo, who came after Candy (the poodle who had been much loved by our midwifery friends). Gismo or Gis for short, our black and tan yorkie-terrier, had a lolling pink tongue and mischievous eyes. She was named after the friendliest gremlin in the pack and soon became part of our family and fitted in with everyone. Soon after Gis arrived we went on our family summer holiday. We sent a card to Sylvia who'd brought Gis to us:

Having a great time. The woods and beach are wonderful.
Lots of places to explore. Enjoying my new family.

Gismo

The reply was that Gis had never been on holiday before and they all hoped he hadn't forgotten his bucket and spade. Gis was not too sure of the sea but digging holes in the sand was great fun and he enjoyed many holidays after that. In spite of a major operation, Gis lived for ten years with us, and was almost fourteen years old when he died. He certainly made his own special contribution to family life with Mum, David and myself at home in Tonyrefail.

25

Trips and Falls
in the parish and nursing homes

THE BIG ADVANTAGE of working in a large parish was that we had two churches almost on the doorstep of the nursing home and they provided us all, nurses and residents alike, with the opportunity to join in with a whole range of activities: home bakes, coffee mornings, concerts, pantomimes and jumble sales all regularly cropped up.

On one particular trip out, everybody was getting ready to return to the home. Nurses and residents all piled into a convoy of cars with matron in front, but on one occasion, her car spluttered and only made brave attempts to get started. You could hear the noise all down the road. Her car wasn't going anywhere. The vicar, who was still inside the church, came out onto the street, now strewn with neighbours and parishioners watching what was going on. Having rallied a few strong men together, they pushed the very full car down a nearby hill where the stubborn engine struggled back to life. I got out of an equally full Robin and joined in to help push and heave. When we all arrived back safely at the nursing home, matron told the story to the waiting members of staff, saying that she looked up from the steering wheel and couldn't believe her eyes. There was the vicar pushing the car, the vicar mind. "Just a minute," I said, "what about me, the curate?"

This humorous event caused so much mirth that we ended up with one case of angina and one asthma attack amongst the residents. We were very used to wheezes and pains and were well equipped when we went out. Once, a humorous entertainer said, "This lady looks ill to me." "Oh I'm alright" she gasped. "You shouldn't be so funny."

When we had more residents needing to go out and more than our cars could cope with, we hired a local minibus to get us around. One time we went to the parish where I'd had my final placement before ordination – the parish where I'd been known for my furry jumpers and balloon-shaped trousers. The most talked about event of the evening however was not totally centred on fun and laughter, but on the handsome vicar, who was the host for the evening. If the church had been a bit nearer to the home then I'm sure he would have had a rapid growth in his congregation, but I fear, for all the wrong reasons. I was questioned for weeks after the event. How long did you say you spent with him? When I replied that it was about ten weeks, they were green with envy.

Christmas pantomimes were always very popular and, with a couple of community theatres nearby, we were all often out late at night. The local bustling shopping centre of Tonypandy, full of bright shop windows and people, had not been visited for a very long time, and often the driver was requested to go around just one more time. We all remembered a very irate 98-year-old who wanted to stay out all night!

Our lives in a busy nursing home often meant squeezing in many and varied activities. On many occasions we were found squashed together, enjoying a shandy or a sherry in the local pub, a coffee in the high street, a walk for some, a push in the wheelchair for others. None of us ever forgot a birthday, and it was always celebrated with a birthday cake and candles, often with visiting family members, a new dress or shirt and an outing planned. When Christmas came around for another year, we inevitably organised a shopping spree.

Parish outings, pub visits and theatre trips with home bakes, raffles, prizes, concerts, shandy and coffee meant we had lots of fun and laughter to share. I have read over the years that laughter gets less frequent as one becomes older. However, I was working amongst some of the most elderly members of the community and hadn't really noticed much difference at all from any other stage in life.

Laughter and fun it seemed, with us anyway, crosses all age barriers and changing my working lifestyle has certainly shown me that. Apart from a lot of fun, there is always a lot of chatter amongst the community of nursing staff and residents. Nurses, it would seem, are capable of talking nonstop, me being no exception to the rule, many would say! There is often a request for yet another story, often followed by a noisy burst of giggles.

After one particular noisy session, one colleague said that she couldn't imagine me being very serious in church. We laugh a lot there as well, I reply, but not usually sharing my stories in the same way, I must admit. The request to tell a story brings up a variety of subjects and events because something seems to be happening all the time. None of our lives stand still, but new experiences take place every moment of the day, even when one is supposedly safe in ones own home.

For example, a couple of men came to our house in Tonyrefail to lay a new carpet. They had covered half the living room when they reached our piano. "Be careful, it's a bit wonky," one of them said. Everything was alright until I passed by just a little too quickly. The piano fell against me, down my left side, clattered onto to my foot and hit the floor with a jangle of keys. "It will have to be tuned now," said Mother. Lifting the heavy instrument off my extremities, the men wanted to send for the doctor. I reassured them that I could check for my own broken bones and they carried on with their work around the room. They both noticed the photograph taken of me with our bishop at my ordination into the diaconate. "Now we know why the air wasn't blue when the piano fell on you," they said. Actually, I just didn't have the breath for the mildest expletive. I couldn't have sworn if I had wanted to! My language can be colourful in two other languages as well as my own, but on that particular day not one of them came to mind. My bruises were viewed with great interest for several weeks to come, almost measuring from the thigh to the ankle according to one member of staff. "Gee Mag," was a comment from one of the nurses. "It's a good job your cassock is long or your congregation would think that you had been beaten up."

A few days after that incident, a heavy chair plus resident landed on my right foot. "For goodness sake, let's hope that is not the piano leg." It wasn't but I was bruised again, needless to say. On another occasion, in the dim light of the stairs, I nearly went head over heels straight to the bottom. A stretched out cat, either Topsy or Turvy was responsible for that bruising. From the heights above came a voice, "Good job you didn't have your cassock on Mag. You could have ended up with more bruises then!"

My bruises kept everybody interested for some time until the subject of cooking came up and I was reminded that, although I had a number of skills, cooking certainly was not one of them. One particular day I launched forth on how to make a luxurious summer pudding using sherry and fruit juice to bind the bread, jelly and fruit together. "How long does it go in the oven for?" asked matron. "Jelly!" we all chorused. Fridge not oven would be a better idea. It took a little while for her to live that one down. However she soon had reason to retaliate. Having seen my lunch of a very battered poached egg on toast and over cooked rice pudding, matron, head cook and staff decided that cooking was not one of my best assets, either. Good job you're not married was the general consensus of opinion. No man would stand much chance of being fed properly, which reminded me of another time and it proved their point. Not so long before this, the vicar in our village had rung me up. "Come up quick," he said, "I've got unexpected visitors." Flinging open his fridge door, he pointed to three large pork chops on a plate. "Cook these," he said, "there are vegetables over there." His face was a picture when I said, "I'd better not. It's either salad or the chippy," the latter proving the favourite. I couldn't hang curtains in his front room either (this was a bachelor vicar, and I the spinster curate). His cryptic comment, asking me what sort of woman I thought I was, didn't inspire me to change, and right up to the present moment I have not improved in either area.

Before I was ordained I had lived in many and varied institutions where I had been well cared for. When I returned to live at home David was a qualified chef amongst other things, and meals were usually ready when I passed in and out. I don't think I have ever cooked pork chops or any other meat without David keeping a watchful eye over me in the kitchen. I have not improved at all and I overheard David say to some friends quite recently, "Margaret is a hopeless cook. I've always got to help her out."

Conversations at work bring up all sorts of subjects and when we talked about nurses' nights out or Christmas celebrations this question always arose. "Are you allowed to come out with us and will the bishop let you come?" I always replied that of course I could come. They could count me in. There ought to be a name for a group of nurses out on the town, like a flock of birds or a gaggle of geese – perhaps a naughtiness of noisy, extrovert and funny ladies. "Right girls," called the entertainer, "up on your feet." Jiving and jigging around, a voice in my ear said, "You couldn't do this in your cassock, Mag." We had a good evening. In fact we had many good nights out in the ten years I worked as a nurse alongside my work in the parishes. After one night out matron, who wasn't with us on that occasion said, "I heard about you and the drink." If I drank a spritzer or a sherry, high jinks were soon to follow. "Just one or two matron!" but I expect it seemed like more than that.

At another time there was an entertainer who was a bit of a one-man band with instruments everywhere: a small keyboard around his neck, cymbals on his elbows, bells at his ankles and a drum kit which he thumped now and again. There was quite a crowd of us out this time, and we were soon up on our feet, with tables and chairs pushed back for more room. By the end of the evening the one-man band was decidedly worn out. "What are you thinking of?" we said, as he was packing up at eleven. "We are night nurses and can carry on all night." "Carry on until 7 a.m.?" he said. "Not even you could help me after that." "Any of your parishioners here Mag?" "I don't think so," I said, which was just as well as my high spirits looked as if they were caused by more than one spritzer or glass of red wine that time. The stories, it seems, are not easily forgotten. The cook at the home must have heard about my red face and high humour after one glass of sherry and, when a party took place in the home, she announced, "Only one glass of sherry for you, Mag."

I was working with a local vicar who was also the chaplain to the local fire brigade. We were invited to spend the evening with them with the vicar blessing the new fire engine and both of us joining the party afterwards. After one sherry I was sternly told that that was quite enough for me. I think now that nurses, cooks and clerics have decided that my high jinks are high enough and have imposed a limit!

All the parties have led to the inevitable need to get slim for the summer with plans to get involved in keep fit, walking, and generally taking care of my health. I had an invitation from some of the ladies in the parish which might have helped me with some of that. "We go tap-dancing every

Tuesday," they said, "come with us." Tap-dancing! I couldn't hide a giggle. Me! Tapping around! I would wreck the class. I had swayed and shaken, in my own way, to the rhythm of the drum and rattles in the Congo but that was my limit, and I was certainly not prepared for the more rhythmic tap which was very popular at the time.

My total inability to conquer that skill didn't deter another group of ladies in the parish from asking me to join them in line dancing. I knew from the very beginning that there was little chance that I was going to cope with that either. However that did not deter any of them and, placing me in the middle amongst the wardens, Sunday school teachers and vicars' wives, a voice hissed in my ear, "Watch me Mag." Slapping their thighs and clicking their heels, they pushed and turned me around with firm hands on my shoulders. All their advice was of little use whatsoever and I inevitably ended up the wrong way round, with all of us collapsing into a hysterical heap. So, I aimed to try something else. "What about swimming?" another enthusiastic group of friends said. I was supposed to be able to swim reasonably well before I went to the Congo. While we were preparing to go, we were all sent to the local swimming baths in Selly Oak, Birmingham for a course of twelve lessons. I did not enjoy it because I never succeeded in staying afloat. It was a lot of fun, but wasted on me I'm afraid.

For life in Africa, it was anticipated that I would be able to swim to a river bank or at least keep myself afloat for a reasonable time until help arrived. But I found out that water snakes and crocodiles were much faster than I would ever be and would easily dispense with me if I had the misfortune to end up in the water. Swimming in the vast Congo river or even a much smaller tributary was just not a good idea for me anyway.

I have tried to learn to swim many times over the years when on holiday. I have endured many a new block of swimming lessons, even trying again when I was retired, but I am very much afraid that my ability to swim is about the same as it was when I first tried it out many years ago.

Tap-dancing, line dancing and swimming were not going to be part of my exercise programme. Then another idea came up, what about a bike? I always wobbled but I had managed to keep myself upright and ride around parts of Cardiff when I was a pupil midwife. I had also enjoyed a few excursions between a few villages in the Congo. This time, I thought, I'll be alright. I'll buy myself a bike.

Unfortunately I still wobbled and was often distracted by passers-by, interested in just me on a bike or wondering what on earth the curate was doing on a bike when she had a nice little car to ride in. The bicycle did help my fitness programme but I tried to keep off the main roads and away from the comments of well-meaning friends. I settled for the easiest kind of bike and thought that I could continue to keep fit without attracting too much attention.

Our dog Gis just loved a long walk and I soon settled for that, setting out for a fairly long walk each day. I found out that Gis was not as gentle as he looked, challenging every other innocent, well-behaved dog for miles around. Even Alsatians and sheepdogs kept their distance: his low, warning growl from somewhere deep in his throat warning them all off. Gis owned the highways and footpaths and, as we belted around the village (it was never a walk), comments such as, "That's a strong little dog" or "Who's taking who for a walk" could be heard. I think we both got fitter and walkies was the easiest exercise of them all. I seemed to have a large blank spot where some things are concerned: cooking, dancing, swimming and bicycling amongst them – my well intentioned efforts causing a great deal of fun all over the place.

I worked in a number of nursing homes during the ten years following my ordination to the diaconate and priesthood. Finally, I worked very close to home in Tonyrefail and close to Mum who, at that time, was still very fit. Mum was still very much part of the community, so much so that the owner at the time asked us both to move in. "So much easier," he said, "and your Mother likes it here." We were not that tempted by the offer. Although I was still very close to the parish I had moved into, Mum would have preferred to stay with David who was just down the road, and that's the way it was in the end.

At one of the nursing homes I worked at the owner decided to buy some animals to keep the residents stimulated and interested. There was no staff meeting or discussion with anybody as there had been when Topsy and Turvy had turned up at another nursing home. These animals just arrived one evening and took up residence in their pre-prepared place, where they could be easily seen and visited by our residents.

I remember one very busy shift. We had a lot more residents to care for than in some of the previous places that I had worked at. Without notice, the owner said to me, "I am going away for three weeks. Can you look after the animals for me?" And he didn't take no for an answer either. However I knew absolutely nothing about the collection of animals he had, and he left no instructions about how to look after them in his haste to get away. Supported and surrounded by the rest of the staff on duty, I decided to phone a local animal advice centre. My first thought had been the vet, but he had had his hands full with Topsy and Turvy and then Gismo, without all these additions too. When I got through to the centre I was asked which animal was I worried about, was it a cat or a dog? It was neither. Instead, I was looking after five goats, fifteen geese, three chickens and what I called a turkey. I later found out that it was a guinea fowl.

There was no response at the end of the phone. Our staff were now giggling behind me. Perhaps the person on the other end thought it was a hoax call. Eventually a voice responded "I'll send you some literature." So, we all had to somehow manage. Initially I went into the enclosure with buckets of food in both hands, but soon beat a hasty retreat from the suspicious goats, spitting geese and screeching fowl. As the days progressed we got used to each other eventually. I was soon surrounded by the now friendly animals, nudging each other out of the way while still hemming me in. I didn't have to make a speedy retreat backwards any more. We were all friends and they followed me to the gate when I left and ran to meet me when feeding time came around again.

We became really close during the next few weeks. The staff and residents watching through the windows commentated that the animals knew me by now. Yes, Dewi, Hughie and Daffodil certainly did. We didn't name the goats, geese, chickens and turkey, only the new baby goats. Eventually an odd-job man was employed to look after the animals as they increased in number, but I still gave them treats and they all still ran to meet me. We had a good shared few weeks together and, with the help of those information sheets and the local farmers, nobody came to any harm. In fact, the owner said that when he returned they all looked considerably better than when he went away.

During the warmer weather, our residents were taken outside to see the antics of the ever-growing family on their very own animal farm. Many of them wanted to make a fuss of them. But, they were all very different from the twin tabby cats in the previous home. Requests to cuddle the chicken or nurse a baby goat were part of our day. With the main gates closed we could let some of them free to run around: baby goats were patted under the watchful eye of the parents who were safely behind the enclosure fence.

"We do have a lot of fun," said one 92-year-old, and the smiling faces and animated expressions showed us how much everybody enjoyed it all. Laughter rang out loud and clear. "Go on, laugh" was often said to me. "We have never heard a laugh like yours before."

My African laugh had survived over many years, loud and long, telling everybody far and wide that happiness spills over in the most surprising places. "You're just the same," friends say to me many years later. "You're ordinary just like us," say my Bible class, and I can't ask for more than that. The mischievous nurse is still very much part of me and so is the adventurous missionary. The fun and laughter is all wrapped up in a night nurses' uniform, most of the time worn in step with a long black cassock.

"Tell us a story," is a request often made over coffee, lunch or in the middle of the night. "We like your stories and we'll listen to them over again." So I rack my brains and inevitably find something to say like:

"I couldn't believe my eyes," said a parishioner looking through her window. "Is that our curate carrying that huge armchair?" "I was lucky" I told her later, "the vicar had the settee."

"You are just no good at moving pianos. Stay in the vicarage. You will only be in the way. You're too small anyway," said the vicar, watched by a small group that had been roped in to move the piano to the church. "Don't you be so sure," I said as I got in the van with the rest of them. "We couldn't have done it without you," they all said later, "those four fingers on the cover made all the difference!" "Well," I told them in work, "I'm not a woman for nothing and all of them were a great deal bigger than me."

Another story went like this: "Whatever happens," I said to Mother, "I must not oversleep in the morning." Setting my alarm clock and checking it carefully, I settled down and was soon fast asleep. Five minutes later, or so it seemed, I was woken up by the harsh ringing of the alarm clock. I staggered out of bed. I thought that I'd had a very bad night.

Barely getting my eyes open I made for the bathroom and gave myself a rousing wash in cold water. Then, downstairs and quite alert by now, I put on the kettle and popped the bread in the toaster. I was beginning to wonder where the daily paper could be. I happened to glance up at the sitting room clock and couldn't believe my eyes. I was well awake by now and it was only half past three. That's why the paper hadn't come, but what had I done to my alarm clock? Never mind, I would go back to bed, leaving a note for David to give me a shout when he got up. I was soon fast asleep. I woke up again, at the right time this time, 6.30 a.m. I washed and dressed again, there was tea and toast again, and a quick glance at the daily newspaper which had arrived this time. I was away and out of the house right on time.

I was telling this tale to women in the church and suggested that I might be quite at home in a community that began their day at 3 a.m. This was greeted with the comments, "Nobody would have you. You are much too noisy, you're better off staying with us," with hoots of laughter of course. The nurses didn't encourage me either, the same tale being greeted with a rousing chorus of: "How do you solve a problem like Maria?" A sort of vicar of Dibley I may be, but a singing nun? Not according to them anyway. But they could be wrong.

*

When we were all training for the ministry, going away on retreat provided a welcome space in a very busy life. We were often joined by students from other walks of life. This particular time there were around twelve of us away together. Meal times were supposed to be silent as most of the days were punctuated by a short prayer and teaching sessions. But, most of the meal times were accompanied by music from a tape deck in a nearby room. We all saw the funny side as television jingles taken from more sober classical music filled the room. Our leader apologised for the noise and breaking the silence; the nuns graciously responded saying that many of the Sisters joined in as well. So you never know. I might not be so out of place after all.

As for me, my two uniforms, nursing and cassock were often worn together or hastily changed from one to another in a choir vestry or nurses' changing room. During the summer I wore quite a feminine blue dress with collar slipped into the neck. "You've got a visitor," called matron down the corridor to one of the residents, one day. On seeing me our parishioner said "Oh, you're the nurse. Have you come to dress my bad leg?" "Not this time," I said, "I've come to see you. I'm your minister." "Well, well," was the reply, "where is your cassock then?" So I put it on, hiding my much cooler dress, so that, in the Rhondda anyway, the roles didn't get mixed up.

Much of the time my clerical clothes have had to go to work too, and it causes some surprise when I come to work in one uniform and leave in another. Once, the painters had been in the nursing home most of the morning, touching up the door frames and skirting boards. They shared our coffee break and chatted to us as we worked our shift. At around two o'clock I went into the changing room and came out in my cassock. The look of amazement was plain for everybody to see as I said "Ta-rah". I didn't have time to explain. I left that to somebody else.

"I have never seen anybody look less like a vicar in all my life," said our secretary in the nursing home when I turned up in jeans, blouse and collar. And what else would I wear to a mother and toddler group, having to spend most of the morning kneeling on the floor? They all approved of my navy blue culottes suit, however. Very smart was the general opinion!

On another day I decided to do some shopping after

conducting a service in the parish church. The busy fruit and vegetable shop became very silent when I walked in. Whatever happened to black? I was clad in pink floral blouse and pink skirt. It seemed a bit of a shock to the locals.

I'm not sure if I was the first female deacon to work in the lower Rhondda but I was certainly amongst the first to be clad like a tropical bird when the valleys had been so used to black or grey amongst the more sober clerical population. Pink in the fruit and vegetable shop and pink (although a variety of other colours had much the same effect) was also worn in church when I lit the candles prior to a morning service. They had never seen pink in such a quantity before they said, but agreed that it was very feminine and cheerful, making a lovely change.

The blouses for lady ministers can be bought in all shapes and sizes, patterns and colours. If what is wanted is not available, material and patterns can be sent off to a variety of clerical firms and made up to order. One telephone call asked me if I wanted frills on the neck and sleeves of all three new blouses. "Better not," I said, "one of them had better be left without," but the pink floral and blue floral are duly frilled at neck and sleeves and they, like most things attached to me, don't go unnoticed.

"I like that," say some, running a finger around the frill. "I've never seen anything like that before." "We can't imagine that under a cassock," say my clerical friends and "Are you allowed to wear those?" from the more cautious. The overall opinion from the parish, especially the women, was very nice and very feminine. And, as I said before, quoting my Roman Catholic nursing friend in the depths of the Congo: "I am a *woman*, after all."

I seem to spend the majority of the time in one uniform or the other and most people expect to see me in one. When occasionally found without either uniform, it's remarked "Oh you've got clothes on," or "Got the sack have you?"

One particular day, the matron went on holiday for three weeks and left me in charge which resulted in me earning quite a bit more money than I usually did. "Treat yourself," said Mother, so I did. We both went on a shopping trip to nearby Cardiff and I returned with quite a smart, up-to-date grey suit. I had a free Sunday evening after this shopping expedition and I thought that I would turn up to church in my new suit. With the long length swirling skirt, short waisted jacket, black leather shoes and frilled blouse (of course), I took my place in the congregation.

I had caused some surprise at the door, greeted with a welcoming "Have a good evening," and was about to be shown to a seat. I stared at the very familiar steward, and he stared at me. "Good gracious," he said, "it's you," apparently unrecognisable in my suit. Somebody else wanted to know where my cassock was and the women thought I looked lovely.

I was really in love with my dual God-chosen role, and between everybody and everything I was enjoying a very special and wonderful time. I would have happily stayed in both roles as was anticipated, but change was once again looming around the corner and I was no stranger to that.

26

Christmas – all over the place

CHRISTMAS IS SUCH a special time and it's not surprising that our Christmas memories go back to the earliest times in our childhood. With only a few years between David and me, we've shared the same lovely recollections together.

When we were children there was always a mince pie and a glass of squash left on the mantelpiece for Santa after his hard work delivering our toys. There were muddy footprints in the passageway and a bowl of water left on the lawn for the reindeer after their flight through the night skies. Dave and I shared the same wonder that Santa had actually been in our house. We remember the shhh… from Mum and Dad going back downstairs when Dave and I were much too excited to go to sleep. Some years later we found out that Dad didn't go to bed at all on Christmas Eve, because sometimes he had a very early shift, starting at 5 a.m. in the local colliery. I don't think Dave and I slept more than a few minutes through our Christmas childhoods. I remember finding a baby doll on the bottom of my bed, the same doll dressed beautifully every Christmas in a complete new outfit lovingly knitted by Mum. David's first train set was also added to, carriage by carriage, every year.

Dave and I grew up on a large council estate in Ty'n-y-bryn, Tonyrefail and Mum saved in a Christmas club all the year round. So we have very traditional memories of fairy lights and a tree, tinsel, trimmings and lametta decorations, chocolates, biscuits, Turkish Delight for Mum and chocolate mints for Dad. There was always turkey, beef, lamb and a nice piece of ham. We always had plenty of food and a houseful of relatives and friends shared our meals. Dave and I have said many times over that Mum and Dad worked an annual Christmas miracle giving us wonderful childhood memories of a very special time.

Christmas changed considerably when David-John appeared on the scene. Of course, it was never the same again. We always had a Christmas tree, dressed with sets of coloured lights. Mum always liked lots of sparkle and the pictures and mirrors were festooned with tinsel. Now we added balloons, chocolate treats and decorations with trains, cars and videos wrapped up as presents under the tree. What a huge difference our very special gift, a newborn baby and growing child made. Before that of course, Christmas had always been hectic with the Reflectors and church friends filling the house. Auntie Lil and Uncle Ernie always joined us on Christmas Eve for sherry and mince pies, as we tucked into the first Christmas dinner of the season.

Candy, our poodle, was with us all then and joined in all the fun with a Christmas stocking full of goodies for herself. I can remember telling one Christmas story about Candy to a group of midwives, one of whom happened to be a very good cartoonist. The story went like this. One particular Christmas I decided to gather together Candy's favourite doggy treats: bones, biscuits, chewy shoes, plastic sausages, all wrapped up in quite a large Christmas parcel. When we were all ready to open our gifts: family, friends, toddler and poodle, all I found of Candy's parcel was an empty packet with the Christmas paper still pretty much intact, but with a convenient hole chewed into the side. Candy had been lifting out and enjoying treats for weeks. She had been having a wonderful time, but there was nothing left on Christmas day. For many years afterwards her gifts were placed on a shelf, well out of her reach. As for my cartoonist colleague, she kept us all amused long after Christmas with doggy pictures of Candy lifting out treats from under the Christmas tree.

Another story comes to mind, when Mum received her Christmas supply of coal. Dad had worked in the colliery above ground for many years, which gave Mum a lovely gift of coal, together with a monthly pension. On this particular day the coal arrived just in time for Christmas. Mum wanted to call David but was unable to attract his attention as he was at the bottom of the garden. I was responsible for David being out of sight however as, some years earlier, I had planted a row of tiny fir trees at the back of the garden alongside the coal shed. Several years later they'd grown to be as tall as the house and from where David was standing, all that could be seen were Mum's spectacles, peering through the branches! I received another series of cartoons of Mum and her glasses trying to attract David's attention amongst the trees. The firs were so thick that I don't think Mum's glasses would have been visible if the sun hadn't been shining on them at the time.

As my days in nursing began I was not able to spend every Christmas day at home – sometimes just a small part of it and memories are interspersed with Christmas fun in the hospital.

Once, we received a letter from the hospital kitchen before Christmas telling us that Christmas dinner would arrive at midday – turkey with all the trimmings. As I was on duty, it was my responsibility to serve Christmas lunch. I was totally horrified and mesmerized to be faced with a whole turkey which had to be carved and served to more than twenty patients and staff. "Move aside," said one of my staff. "I'll carve, you serve the sprouts."

Christmas of course is all about a very special baby born to us on Christmas Day, and of course maternity units and midwives everywhere long to safely deliver a Christmas baby. Oh, what joy to families, friends and staff as the new arrival is gently placed in a specially prepared Christmas cot, lovingly decorated weeks before by a member of staff with an artistic talent. The finished creation can rival any to be found in a baby shop, as it is resplendent with net tulle and satin bows. Of course only the first baby born on Christmas Day could be placed in the Christmas cot. Any others following, as there often were, were placed in the everyday nursery equipment. There were special decorations and presents for all of them, but only the first one enjoyed the very splendid Christmas cot.

I am reminded of the year I had two Christmases, one at home and one in Belgium spent with many special people who launched me on my very busy life to come. I have precious and personal memories of Belgium and the Russian friends and the Christmas they shared with me.

The Christmases in the Congo are particularly treasured and remembered as if they happened yesterday. Christmas in equatorial Africa turned everything on its head. Letters I had written in 1969 and 1970 remind me of how very different my life had become in a far distant place. I remember the 100°F heat and the moist sticky air of the tropics. Memories stay with me of carol singers coming up my path as dawn was breaking. Some years there'd be a sudden tropical storm on Christmas Day. But, the sky would soon clear enabling us all to enjoy our Christmas meal outside. We were joined by all our mission workers and their families, sometimes several hundred in number. There was football on the field and I often had to remind myself that I was only supposed to kick the ball from the sidelines and not join in the scrum in the middle of the field!

I never knew what I was eating for any meal, let alone the Christmas meal. One time a dead large hairy gorilla was seen straddled across a bicycle. I did wonder if that could be part of dinner. Sometimes I'd see a crocodile and that was a wonderful lunch. We were in the middle of a biblical miracle; we were in one of the poorest places on earth, yet everybody was just about fed.

I well remember the year when we received a letter from government officials giving us permission to shoot and eat an elephant. "You are so many now," said the letter "this large animal will feed you all." None of us had the heart to do as the letter advised. There was one very lucky elephant roaming around somewhere in the heart of the forest that particular Christmas of 1969.

Letters remind me that I wrote about the church packed to the rafters with the harmonious singing of many choirs, hand clapping, foot shuffling, glass tinkling and a drum proclaiming the news out far and wide that Jesus Christ had been born on this day.

Christmas dinner was always followed by dancing accompanied by wide infectious smiles and children running and playing. There were no presents as there was nothing to give each other on this special day except the gift of oneself in friendship, love and care, a gift I have treasured all my life.

I remember that three new babies born on Christmas day in the Congo and I remember the little baby boy who died. I will never forget the heartbreaking wailing as the family returned to their village.

The only present I could send home to Mum, just one gift in four years. The female students and Pauline who lived with me, cut out a square of white material, trimmed it with a colourful edging and I managed to embroider 'Mum' in the middle. I have that with me now, more precious memories woven into the fabric of my life.

Returning back home to Wales, Christmas took on its usual frantic pattern but for years to come I longed for the tropical Christmas and longed for the noise of the African hospital and so many friends. However Christmas celebrations resumed with a vengeance with many wonderful people and one advantage being that in Wales at least I did know what I was eating!

New Christmas memories came about as I found myself in a busy lively parish in Llantrisant. The three day Christmas tree festival there saw fairy lights and decorations and many varieties of trees from fifty-three areas of parish and community life. It was joyous to see over 1,000 people passing through the ancient church enjoying choir singing and presentations from surrounding schools. Santa in his grotto, flanked by elves and angels was a firm favourite, with excited children whispering wishes and clutching presents. In 2008, BBC Wales broadcasted live from the church, interviewing a teacher and children from a local school who had decorated their own tree. Warm mulled wine, fairy cakes, sandwiches and hot tea was in constant supply and made our parish Christmas very welcoming and special.

I am reminded of the first Christmas for our Caitlin. She was three months old and resplendent in a white satin dress and red silk bows. That year I bought a small Christmas tree in a pot. It was about 8 inches tall, covered in spray snow and a few decorations. In the new year I planted the tiny tree in a larger pot with fresh compost, and watered it regularly. I didn't really notice it growing so fast, until it needed a large pot and was several inches higher. I transferred it and soon friends were saying that the tree should be put in the garden, which is exactly what I did. We all thought a reasonably-sized Christmas tree would develop. After a couple of years in the garden it was now over 5 foot tall. Caitlin slept a cabin bed with fairy castle and slide which elevated her to window level; from three years of age she watched the tree grow and three years later it was parallel with her bedroom window. Downstairs, it was a different story. The trunk was waist width and the branches filled the conservatory window and blocked out all the light. A new gardener came to plant some fruit bushes for David and was amazed to see this very large tree in our back garden. "What on earth is that doing here?" he asked giving it a long complicated name with many syllables. "It belongs in the forest."

When I told him I had bought it seven years earlier as a tiny tree decoration he was totally amazed. "You should not have planted it in a domestic garden. The roots will shake the foundations; it will have to come down." I related this tale to the greengrocer up the road where I had bought the tree. "You've had your money's worth," he said, "I should have charged you more!" Robert, the gardener, said that they were only sold as small branches for Christmas decoration and that it wouldn't have entered anybody else's head to plant it in a small back garden. But, I did! Caitlin still reminds me of the Christmas when I cut my tree down.

Christmas memories tumble over one another: painful and joyous, tear soaked and filled with laughter, noisy crowds and grieving families. Christmas nevertheless brings its own special worldwide gift of peace and joy.

Reading a prayer letter from Africa in 1970, I quote the words that Jesus was not born into snow and ice, trimmings and affluence. He came in overwhelming heat, poverty, illiteracy and ignorance and exposed to the vast differences between rich and poor. He came to all mankind, God's people everywhere, with a very special Christmas message of love, joy and peace.

27

Priesthood

MY TRAINING FOR ordination was sometimes long and difficult and extended over a four year period and was combined with working in a busy profession. However once in the parish I embraced my new life with much joy. The pieces of my life were fitting together with an uncanny familiarity.

In the Anglican tradition, priesthood follows a probationary year served in the diaconate. For centuries this had only been open to the male population. Nevertheless changes were taking place and our church, which had ordained women to the diaconate for many years, wrestled with the question of ordaining women (of which there were a large number by now), into the priesthood.

I struggled with the same questions. I examined the same doubts, deciding initially that I was content and complete where I was. I think I probably would have stayed that way, but the pressure exerted in this corner of a very traditional Rhondda background, caused me to examine the issue with greater depth and clarity.

I thought of all the other times when I hadn't measured up – I'd failed the 11+ for example. "You'll never make it." "A trained nurse?" "Africa? What's got into her head now?" "A teacher?!" I thought of all the pessimism, some of the difficulties and much discouragement at major crossroads. Then I thought of God and my Saviour Jesus, who had stood by me at ten years of age and had never left my side. God had made all the choices before and he would do the same now.

I did not actively support any pressure groups or single-sex gatherings. I had always worked freely and easily with my male and female colleagues, getting on with God's work. Consequently I decided to leave well alone and, in God's good time, let it work itself out.

During this time I read relevant articles and books and with much specific prayer, tried to understand the different spiritual areas and traditions, discussions, arguments, debates and personal pain of opposing areas.

During the three and half years in the diaconate I celebrated the Eucharist alongside the priest in charge. Then, I came across a book written by the late Michael Ramsey, *The Christian Priest Today*, a series of addresses given to those about to be ordained priest and deacon. I quote the words which were relevant to where I had come from and where I was going: "You will find yourself as celebrant at the Eucharist privileged with a unique intensity to be with God and with the people in your heart. There is no separated realm of piety; the Christ who feeds them is at one with the pain of humanity around them." Reflecting on my long spiritual journey I knew that I could not be separated from the most precious and holy part of Christian ministry.

With the same amazement I experienced when I was ordained into the diaconate, I took my place in the cathedral and was ordained alongside many other female deacons into the priesthood on the 11th of January 1997.

The deep, complete joy of celebrating the Eucharist with God's people embedded into my heart and connecting with suffering humanity, brought me full circle. I remained in the self-supporting ministry and continued nursing. Content that God knew best, He had charted every step, from my baptism as a young child to an adult more than forty years later.

My mirror image of early training for mission was brighter and my circle was complete. My two lives had merged together smoothly and perfectly and, as I looked back on it all, I was totally amazed, and said words that I'm sure I have said before:

"Only God could do that."

28

Another Parish

I worked at St John's and St Luke's churches in the parishes of Porth with Llwyncelyn for three and a half years. I loved my role in the diaconate, working in the community and alongside the priest on Sundays and some weekdays.

My hectic life was beginning to become more like my life in Africa. I was often asked if I would like a parish of my own and receive a stipend (wage) for my work. I decided against this as moving between parish and nursing was rooted in my early life. Leaving nursing didn't fit easily with me. Later, I moved down the road, so to speak, and my life took on a whole new dimension as I became an ordained priest in Hopkinstown with Maesycoed, Pontypridd.

When I arrived there I must have mentioned that I could play the piano with music. Soon, an electronic piano arrived which I had agreed to try out before one of the services started. According to the vicar and all those coming into the service, I was doing fine, and it was lovely to sing the hymns to music. It didn't stay like that for long, needless to say, because behind me stood a large two keyboard organ with pedals and many stops, most of which I didn't understand. I was then subject to various degrees of pressure: "Go on, you can do it." "Gold star for you if you play the organ." "Have a try." Never being one to cower from a challenge, I haphazardly pulled out a selection of stops until I found a reasonable noise, and ignoring the pedals and with a familiar hymn, set forth. Musical strains brought the vicar out of his vestry and wardens stopped in their tracks. "Lovely", they all agreed, "just right for Sunday". I had earned my gold star and gained yet another job amongst many others.

The services went very well while I was finding my feet in the new parish and with a new vicar. Blissful uncomplicated days were shared together but that situation would not last very long. Now ordained into the priesthood I could launch out on my own, the vicar and myself sharing three congregations and often working at opposite ends of the parish. Sundays were very busy. Now I had to do all the work on my own, but our lovely congregation (now used to the organ) were not prepared to accept that. Sundays were hectic as I frequently moved from organ to lectern, pulpit to organ, lectern to altar and back to the organ.

Nobody minded and it didn't take long for me to realise that the congregation were having a great deal of fun at my expense. Being five foot and a bit, it appeared that I regularly disappeared in my journey through the service. Sharing the peace was accompanied by wide smiles if not wide grins all around me. I have always stood on a stool in our high Welsh pulpits, otherwise I would just be a disembodied voice, but nothing could be done about me completely disappearing from view when sat at the organ and reappearing again all over the place minutes later, only to disappear again for the next hymn. I threatened them all that I would shut the cover for good and get the piano out. "Don't do that," they said. "We haven't enjoyed ourselves so much for a long time." I don't think the vicar even found out about our Sunday fun – after all he was always somewhere else.

My frantic combined existence continued for some considerable time until a young man in the congregation brought some order and said, "I can't sit here any longer watching you rushing around. I'll play for you." Lovely! What a change! My appearing and disappearing act, like a jack-in-the-box was over; so was the fun, although I have never lived it down.

St David's, the largest of the three churches, was in the middle of a very supportive community and regularly conducted bazaars, Christmas parties, concerts, craft fairs and open days with ice cream vans and bouncy castles that brought lots of children and young people to us. "Let's have a youth club," was the suggestion and with Maureen Lewis and Mary Wiltshire and many other helpful pairs of hands, we opened up with a tuck shop, games and handicrafts which soon proved popular with a large group of young people children and their parents. Mary had previously worked as a commissioner with the Girl Guides and Maureen as a keep fit/dance teacher. Soon twenty or so youngsters were siphoned off from the larger group into keep fit, dance and crafts.

This launched us into a number of events which joined up with many other groups in the Rhondda. Our young people became part of a larger display of dancing and exercise, for example. Soon we were invited to do a show for Easter and Christmas which involved many months of preparation and dressmaking. It was suggested that we should have a name and a costume. Sitting the group all down with pencils and large sheets of paper, we set about to choosing a name and design.

We unanimously agreed to be called Joybells, and pictures of smiley faces on yellow shirts with red peaked caps completed the picture. They were soon turned into T-shirts and headgear and we were ready for our first family service and show. Probably our most ambitious project was a production of *Joseph and his Technicolour Dreamcoat*. Sometimes we wrote our own musicals, all choreographed by Maureen, Mary and I. Joybells excelled themselves in their presentation of the musical *Grease* and did even better with *Sister Act* which proved very popular all round, and that was the only occasion when I became a singing nun, which might have been wishful thinking some time before.

"The bishop is coming for the confirmation service," said the vicar during one Friday evening. "The Joybells can do a presentation while the altar is being prepared. The bishop will have moved up to the altar by then so you will have plenty of room above the chancel steps." I cued the music and the Joybells waited in front of a very large congregation to begin an enthusiastic singing and dance routine. However the bishop hadn't moved and of course neither had his chair. The children however were not to be outdone and, as the music played, they danced and sang all around the bishop in a greatly reduced space until the item was over. It didn't faze them at all.

Nobody had seen anything like this as an introduction to a confirmation service before, which didn't surprise any of us one bit. Everybody was totally delighted with our Joybells, who had exceeded themselves on that special evening. They also entertained us at several of Mum's birthday parties when a particular dance was set to a lively number sung by Sir Cliff Richard – Mum loved that. Joybells brought her much joy on her ninetieth and ninety-third birthdays. As our family grew bigger, subsequent birthdays right up to ninety-seven years of age were celebrated at home.

Fun was very much part of the five years Joybells spent together, with them being the highlight of our church fellowship and community, giving us all many happy memories for the rest of our lives.

2 9

Cruse Bereavement Care

MUM STAYED IN very good health, having never been ill or in hospital in our lifetime. We had a wonderful celebration for her ninetieth birthday in a local church hall where I was the curate at the time. We had caterers, a glass of wine for every guest on arrival and over a hundred family and friends joined us. David iced a wonderful birthday cake and proudly walked with Mum to meet and greet every guest.

As mentioned, the Joybells entertained us, and Mum shared her lifelong testimony of faith in Jesus Christ with us all. Mum had been baptised by total immersion when she was fourteen years of age and could clearly testify to the love and devotion she had experienced all her life, knowing that Jesus Christ was her Saviour and Lord. We had more parties every year for the next three years of her nineties, and I continued my dual role as curate and nurse and David worked at the Royal Mint.

Mum was still very busy, enjoying her life with many activities in church and the nursing home where she became a popular figure. On reaching ninety-five years of age, everybody agreed that she was very well for her age.

Then one afternoon, in the middle of summer, I came home from work to find her very unwell and her lunch untouched. The doctor said that her heart had become very irregular and that had caused her to faint. Mum soon recovered with the help of medication and in spite of several short hospital admissions, she continued to enjoy a good quality of life.

For the next year or so, I stopped working in the parish and nursing home. David stayed in work and between us we managed quite well. Although slower, Mum could still walk to the car, my small Robin Reliant and also to Dave's more comfortable Vauxhall Viva. We had trips out to the seaside, country parks, and restaurants and to family and friends, often taking Blaze our whippet when visiting the family in Cardiff. The time passed quickly and Mum celebrated another Christmas with four-year-old Caitlin and then her ninety-seventh birthday.

A lady called Rosemary Ashman from our parish church shared house communion with Mum and me once a month. Mum sat in our bay window and waved to people passing, always observant of the bus queues forming outside our gate as they waited for the hourly bus service to Cardiff. As Rosemary prepared Communion she asked Mum if she would like to read the scripture passage. None of us at that time had any idea that our beloved Mum would soon be leaving us. Mum's voice rang out loud and clear reading from Habakkuk, who trusts in God's salvation. I can hear Mum reading those words now:

Hab 3:17–19
Although the fig tree shall not blossom, neither shall fruit be on the vines; the labour of the olive shall fail, and the fields shall yield no meat; the flock shall be cut off from the fold, and there shall be no herd in the stalls:

Yet I will rejoice in the Lord, I will be joyful in the God of my salvation.

The Lord God is my strength, and he will make my feet like hinds' feet, and he will make me to walk in high places.

A few days after the Communion, Mum unexpectedly collapsed and spent her remaining days in the local hospital. Mum received the last offices and final prayers, then rallied and chatted to us all with Caitlin sitting on her bed. Then, Mum lapsed into a deep coma, going home to God, to her Saviour Jesus who she had loved for so long, only fourteen days after taking Communion and reading those stirring verses from the prophet Habakkuk.

David and I sat with Mum in the last hours of her life. She still looked well and was peacefully asleep. The nurses came to care for her at midnight and left us alone when they heard Dave and me saying our final prayers and committing our beloved Mum into the hands of God.

We were left quietly to sit with Mum. I washed her hands and face and brushed her hair, laying out her very best silk nightgown. Dave and I reflected on a very special Mother who had held us altogether, creating a bond of love between us all that will never be broken. We left her in the early hours of the morning, heartbroken yes, but giving thanks to God for a very special person: our Mum.

Mum was brought home to rest in the parish church at the same time as a meeting of the ladies group. The leader apologized to me and said perhaps they had better go home. Not at all, we said. Mum was always in a party, if not her own, somebody else's and was certainly always in a crowd of people. Why should anything alter now? It was so typical of Mum to be close to people; why should anything change in her death? As in life, our Mum was left in God's care surrounded by people who knew her so well and were a great comfort to us all at this painful time. Mum's wishes were that she be cremated and laid to rest with Dad, her beloved husband, who had left us so early, thirty-three years earlier.

I was asked if I would like to lay her ashes to rest and, on a very sunny morning in late September 2004, I agreed to do that.

Vi Griffiths, my dear friend who had walked every step of the way, was with me, joining me in the cemetery. I held

Mum's earthly remains close to my chest, Vi and I reading the newly inscribed plaque. Mum was almost ninety-eight years of age and had left her earthly home for heaven, resting now peacefully with Dad.

I read her favourite, Psalm 121:

I will lift up mine eyes unto the hills from whence cometh my help. My help cometh from the Lord who made heaven and earth. The Lord shall preserve thy going out and thy coming in from this time forth and forevermore.

We said the 'Lord's Prayer' together and left with our memories of a very precious Mum and Dad.

Mum had asked me when she was around eighty years old and still out preaching every Sunday, not to say 'died' when her obituary notice was written and funeral service conducted. Say: "I've been folded into God's embrace." Dave and I repeated her request to the undertaker and newspaper. We later found that her will and letters to us and funeral arrangements had all been revised and completed when she was eighty. Mum was ready then but had never considered it as an ending, always living as Dad did with the hope of heaven in her heart. Going to sleep in this world and waking up with God was a natural transition, living and dying being an unbroken continuous line. Coming to a full stop was never considered.

Mum and Dad share the same plaque and text which she had chosen for Dad so many years before:

I have fought the fight; I have kept the faith.

As I celebrate Communion now, I often think of our beloved parents when the church militant here on earth joins the church triumphant in heaven saying together:

Now with all the Angels and Archangels and all the Company
of Heaven we laud and magnify your glorious name, Amen.

Some weeks later I realised that I was not well. I was
heartbroken in church each Sunday and I plunged into a
deep grief as the services continued. I went to visit my doctor
who said that if I didn't feel any better to come and see him
in a month.

The long hours Mum and I had shared together were now
a gaping black hole and I gazed into agonising darkness that
nothing else it seemed would fill. Mum had contacted Cruse
Bereavement Society when Dad had died and now I decided
to do the same. Life seemed to have ground to a halt.

During the few short years since Mum died, I have often
shared the words of Jesus to the widow of Nain over the
death of her son. Agonising blackness probably wouldn't
have been strong enough words to describe how she felt
too. A widow, with no means of supporting herself, was left
totally alone when her only son died. When Jesus saw her
he had compassion for her and said, "Don't cry". With those
words Jesus brought light into darkness, life into death and
hope into hopelessness, restoring a son back to life to his
mother.

Sometimes I feel that Mum is so close, almost looking
over my shoulder, still taking an interest in all that is going
on in my life. My tears still flow and then I am reminded
of the words of Jesus, "Don't cry", bringing light to life and
hope to me and all those who are bereaved. Heaven is not
very far away, and one day all our loved ones will be gazing
over the balcony of heaven ready to welcome us home, to
that eternal place where there will be no more tears, no
more weeping, no more painful partings again.

As I said, after Mum died, life for me ground to a stop.
Having retired from the nursing home and parish, I had no
organisation that I could return to as I did when Dad passed

away. The last year that Mum and I had shared together had been full of bright spots of happy memories, but now after her death, many hours mounted up, blank and empty.

I was greeted by a friendly voice at Cruse Bereavement Care. And, after a couple of conversations I was invited to go to Cardiff to meet some of them working there. I soon found out that the voice on the phone belonged to Rhian Pate, who had trained as a pupil midwife with me in Cardiff forty years earlier. I joined a small group for an hour a week. During that time I began to learn about the organization and found out about how it all began.

The mission statement of Cruse says that bereavement care exists to promote the wellbeing of bereaved people and to enable anyone suffering bereavement to understand their grief and cope with their loss. This statement has forty years of work behind it and the origin of the word Cruse comes from the Old Testament story of Elijah who, when visiting a widow, asked her to supply him with some oil taken from her cruse, an earthenware pot. Little remained, but, because she was willing to share this with the prophet, it never ran out again. Cruse is not an organization built on any particular religion; people of all faiths and none at all are welcomed as service users, volunteers and staff. Although originally a service for widows, Cruse could not fail to notice the problems experienced by many other groups including children or anyone experiencing loss or grief. Today Cruse Bereavement Care exists to provide information and support to anyone bereaved by death.

Coming to the end of the year with, what turned into a lively and very friendly group, I was asked if I would like to stay and join in many of the branch activities. If I had previously thought that the pace of my life had reduced to nothing, then I was greatly mistaken. Every Monday for the next couple of years saw me first acting as a supporter, then leader of the friendship group.

Here, a large group of people that were affected by bereavement met for a coffee and a chat. Soon we were all enjoying days out, most days flashing our bus passes at bemused bus drivers and travelling all over the place for free. We planned Christmas parties and Christmas dinners in the nearby Hilton hotel. We celebrated many birthdays, out and about, all crammed between weekly meetings.

I began to enjoy every minute and wasn't too surprised when another suggestion was soon made. "How would you like to train as one of our counsellors?" I was asked. It involved several months of training which were held on weekends and evenings. But, I had no intention of becoming so involved. Nevertheless, I did turn up and joined a class of fifteen students who were years younger than myself.

On the first weekend I looked comfortable, even smart, much like the tutor I had been, and dressed suitably for my advancing age. Looking around at my peers, I saw a very different image, most being from a variety of different professions to which they would return when the course was over. So, the following weekend saw me changed from skirts, small heels and coloured jumpers, into faded jeans, trainers and a sweatshirt. I would have loved a sparkly scarf in my hair or around my waist, dangly earrings and violet nails, but not even I could get away with that!

I found that the course involved quite a lot of casework study and self-awareness. It reflected often on my African background, nursing, midwifery, ordination and pastoral work, but still, I came to the conclusion that I had loads to learn.

I was now becoming very busy again with Mondays and weekends taken care of. I thoroughly enjoyed the training course, as I made new friends and enjoyed an end-of-course party, once again receiving another certificate to paper my walls. As a volunteer with the Monday friendship group, a deep void in my life had begun to fill up.

I was now able to meet people who came to Cruse for bereavement support. After all my years in many and varied situations my feelings, as I waited for my first client, were indescribable. Here I was launching out yet again on another two full years of supervised training with deadlines to meet each month and standards to maintain. I was very wrapped up in it all and found time to recognise that life was improving and that I was enjoying every minute of it once again.

As I shared many people's troubles, I had time to reflect on my sorrows as well. I remembered the terrible disappointment of never returning to Africa and a busy, almost continuous student existence broken up by periods of ill health. I reflected on the shattering loss of my beloved Dad, David's serious illness and his divorce and return home to me. My bouts of migraine persisted for many long years; they were distressing and debilitating causing concern during pre-ordination training. The difficult periods seemed to continue relentlessly.

Then, things began to come together which had given me a new lease of life. I attended a church retreat and during that time we were asked if we would like healing, and if so, to go to the priest who would give us holy water which we were to place on the affected part. My turn came and I threw my share all over my head, not at all gently or prayerfully, more as a plea to get rid of my condition. Miraculously, after almost twenty years of migraines, which had been aggravated by living and working in the Congo, the headaches stopped and now, more than ten years later, the episodes have never been repeated, not even the simplest headache.

Then a little while later, my optician prescribed a new combination of distance, bifocal and shade and reading glasses for study. Now ten years later, my eyes are improving and, being well into pensioner's age, I have no migraines, no headaches and my eyesight is clearer now than it has ever been. As I've said before, doing things upside down or back to front seems to be very much a part of my life.

By this time in my life, I had caught up with so many friends whose lives had been changed by bereavement or health issues and having to start again. Sharing experiences with them eased the painful parting from Mum and the huge gap left after many years together.

Most people in Cruse knew that I was also an ordained Anglican priest but not all knew about that vital part of my life. "Can you make it by 12.15 p.m.?" I was asked over the phone. "I'll be there," I said. In between I had some unexpected work to do in the parish and another hour had to be filled in. I rang ahead to say that I would be late.

What they were not prepared for was me turning up in full clerical clothes, cassock and collar, having not had the time to change. They looked on as I stepped out of the cassock. (I never undo all those little buttons!) "Just look at what she's got on underneath," was the comment... jeans!

I said, "Count yourself lucky. On a warm day I wear a lot less."

Some other friends wonder, four years down the line, why I am still there. I reply, "I want to see everybody who comes." Bereavement touches us all, ignoring race, creed, religion or faith. We all feel the same pain. I want to be with them all.

Life with Cruse is a little less frantic now. I am able to travel to Cardiff several times a week. The bus pass is always at the ready. I enjoy lunch out, meet a friend, and wander around the shops. This is a good time. A time for space, listening, healing and new beginnings, new friendships and none of us can be too old for that.

30

A Hospital Chaplain

IN APRIL 2005 I was present at the Maundy Thursday service at our mother church, Llandaff Cathedral. The bishop's chaplain requested a word with me before I returned home. "Would you like to go to the Prince Charles Hospital in Merthyr Tydfil and work as their hospital chaplain for about three months?" he asked.

It meant going back to the hospital where I had worked as a tutor and midwife. What a surprise and just as I had said "yes" to Cruse on Mondays, I said "yes" to chaplaincy for a three-day working week. Therefore, in a short space of time I was immersed in a four-day week and also busy in the parish on Sundays – my life was filling up once again.

"I don't know quite where to start with you," said my line manager as we met each other at the Prince Charles Hospital. Hospital chaplains at this time (2005–06), were being employed and salaried as a working partner in a hospital environment. Visiting ministers from their local areas were a valuable part of the team also, and I suppose I was a bridge between the two. "Oh, just employ me like a midwife," I replied and, for the first time in fifteen years, I received a salary in a ministerial capacity. I was back in the same areas as I had worked in while preparing for ordination. "By the way," they said "do you still drive that three-wheeler car?"

"What would you like me to wear?" I asked. "Much the

same as us," was the reply. I was comfortable in short-sleeved jackets, floral skirts and a selection of coloured clerical blouses. "Very cheerful," were the comments passed as I made my way around the 800-bed hospital.

"Three months should be enough," said the bishop's chaplain. "We are so glad to have your help." However, things didn't quite work out that way, but when did anything go to plan in my busy life? Hospital chaplaincy would not be the exception.

Robin and I, my faithful three-wheeler friend, set out on the twenty-five mile journey at 7 a.m. each morning and returned at 5 p.m. each evening. I arrived to a cheery "Good morning" from the hospital porters, and then went up a flight of stairs to the chapel. After opening the post, I welcomed the first visitors of the day.

Some visitors stayed for a quick chat; others for morning prayer and several to weekly Communion. Since the chapel was on the main hospital corridor, many stopped by to say hello, adding, "I couldn't believe my eyes. When did you get back?" News travelled like wildfire and soon I was invited to coffee all over the place, especially with the midwives I had worked with so long ago.

I had completely underestimated my feelings when I saw a baby, just born a few minutes earlier, placed in its cot. I had to fight with my instincts not to pick the baby up, feel him snuggle into my neck and breathe in the scent that only comes with a new life. Sadly, I wasn't the midwife now. I was back in very familiar territory alongside the profession which I had loved and worked in all my life. But I was the hospital chaplain now and I had many other areas in the hospital to visit and work in also.

At least the midwives could see that all the hard work had paid off. The self-supporting minister doesn't wake up to morning prayers and breakfast as in a college environment but wakes up at 5.30 a.m., travels and, if a midwife like me, delivers a baby and works on the wards before the day has barely begun.

Most of my colleagues had been at my ordination. I couldn't have achieved that without their support and friendship. The midwife was still there in me, as I discovered when I found myself on the maternity unit. On occasions I would hear the words, "Oh! Never mind your collar. We are short of staff!"

How I would have loved to have got back into the thick of it all but the Reverend Margaret Maund was on duty now, and had a very new job to get used to.

I was at the beginning of a very busy year. A year? Oh yes! A year would pass before the new chaplain would take over. Meanwhile I was having a wonderful time and enjoying every minute of it all.

There were smaller medical units some distance away: a kidney dialysis centre and a mental health unit. My life was now almost totally pastoral, much the same as a parish, but now hospital-based with the addition of interfaith activities, coronary and intensive care, special care baby units and visiting patients preparing for surgery. Sadly many patients died and I was back preparing for funerals, visiting the families, all of whom became friends.

I also visited the very large catering department and was taken to meet the senior catering manager. I can still see the look of shock on his face when he was faced with a clerical-collared female heavily clad in pink. I don't think an equivalent had knocked on his office door before. We talked about menus, the availability of specific food in a 24-hour seven-day-a-week service, including fasting and dietary provisions in a multifaith community.

In a large hospital with an active interfaith community, I soon found myself chatting to and visiting representatives and employees of many faiths. This was a valuable time for me and the experiences I gained enriched my life. Memories now tumble into each other. I recall passing a group of colleagues going to an update lecture in maternity care. It provoked the comment: "Oh, come with us Mag. Nobody will notice the difference." Several months down the line, I was not at all sure about that. There were many happy hours spent in the outpatient departments and emergency areas, where I often joined groups and patients for coffee and Welsh cakes.

I was also integrated into the local churches and was invited by the priests to join a barbecue, a special service or a function. I was still in the hospital to celebrate Christmas which was wonderful, especially with the children sharing Christingles of oranges and sweets, red ribbons and a lighted candle telling us all that Christ was born on this special day.

The summer months were now approaching fast and, in a change of clothes, I looked a little different a year down the line, as I had gained three extra stone in one year. Not at all surprising really, as I had enjoyed every pound gained. Nevertheless enough was enough, time was marching on and my knees were painful and my cassock was bursting at the seams. So, soon after my departure, I joined a weight reducing class. "Tell us Margaret why you have found us," said the group leader. "I am three stone overweight" I responded "and my cassock won't fit." Thirty blank stares met my gaze with the question, "What's a cassock?" They were soon to find that priests also get heavy.

Conversations immediately took the same turn as they always did. "What do I do about this? How do I get in touch with the vicar – but, can you do it instead?" I was still very busy in my self-supporting/missionary role. Nothing had changed at all since I had first set foot in my beloved Africa. My life as an Anglican priest at home in south Wales was no different in many ways.

31

A New Parish

IN THE SUMMER of 2007 my life as hospital chaplain came to an end. However my work with Cruse continued and now extended into visiting clients in prison. This involved yet another course on prison awareness. My clients were referred from the many and varied areas of prison life, and people who were experiencing the pain and personal loss of bereavement.

At this time, I was worshipping in my home parish of Tonyrefail when our assistant bishop came up with a surprising suggestion. "How about retiring to Llantrisant?" he said, "and you can join in from time to time if you wish." As I was now past church retirement age and had been flashing my bus pass around for several years, I thought it was a very good suggestion. "I will tell the vicar that you will be there soon," was his response. I turned up the following Sunday. "This is my friend Margaret," said Viv the vicar to the large congregation. Viv and I had been ordained together and knew each other quite well. "Margaret will be sharing the services from time to time," he continued, "but she is retired, so, most of the time she will be sitting in the congregation with you."

That proved to be an understatement in itself! Nobody could have seen what lay ahead then, least of all me. I was soon in the midst of a church with a Sunday school, very busy youth clubs and Alpha groups. There was a crowd of women in Mother's Union, and an equally large crowd of women who lunched. I was invited to join them all. Then another suggestion came from another group of women. "We would like a Bible study too, but can't get out in the evening." And with those words, ABC was launched (Afternoon Bible Club) with monthly visits and social activities.

A couple of services later, Viv asked me if I would like to join the monthly rota. That began a whole new series of experiences sharing three churches on Sundays and during the week. I was delighted to follow black leather-clad Ian, our assistant curate, and his large motorbike around, and loved being part of the team. I do sometimes sit in the congregation, but not nearly as much as I'd anticipated at the beginning.

Along with the introduction, "This is my friend Margaret," came a question from the sideman on the door. "Don't you walk your dog around the park?" I was a bit mystified as, although I was not too far from home – about four miles, there were several parks in between.

A little while later, Viv the vicar explained. "That's Rob," he said, "he teaches at Tonyrefail School and his classroom overlooks the park." I was interested now and felt more than a little foolish when I turned up to preach my first sermon. The sideman had now become crucifer and sacristan and was sitting in the lectern opposite me. Viv roared with laughter when I told him that I did walk the dog around the park most days of the week but that when I said walk, it wasn't strictly true because I used the park as a gym (after all it is free).

There are several areas of raised ground in our park with many bushes and trees, a leisure centre and library, together with three entrances and exits. Blaze and I belt around the lot, up and down, in and out, appearing and disappearing, passing a very hectic hour or more, all viewed sometimes apparently from the classroom above the park.

I laughed with Viv, but he soon wiped the smile off my face. "Rob is a Head of French." Memories resurfaced of all those other Heads of Department whose French language classes I had passed through – post Blaugies and post Bruxelles, who were horrified without exception every time I opened my mouth. "You have a wide vocabulary" was always the comment, "but where on earth did you get an accent like that?"

This time I would not be airing any language other than English and at that time there was no reason why I should. Somehow or other, as time passed by, the odd French phrase slipped in. To my surprise it was considered not bad at all.

*

Robin, my three-wheeler, faithfully took me back and forth around the parish, until it developed a whole host of mechanical problems, not helped by a spate of vandalism in our village at the time. There were no buses on a Sunday and my life down the road looked set to reach an unhappy end almost before it had begun.

"You're having a lot of bad luck with that," said some. And others said, "You've got the devil on your back!" I laid my hand on the badly scarred roof and prayed, "If I'm staying in Llantrisant, Lord, something has got to be done about this car." In the months that followed precious friends picked me up, with David often running me home after a service. "Ring me up, I'll help you out," and between everyone they made sure I didn't miss a thing and I kept my place on the parish rota.

Robin my Reliant friend is fine at the moment and I've learned that, whatever the circumstances, when things go wrong, God's people are exactly the same wherever they are, stepping in, offering help and friendship, standing alongside and in the process, increasing our faith.

I balance parish life and Cruse, now comfortably functioning alongside each other and, as I look back on the last few years, I pose the question: Retirement, what's that?

32

The End?
Or, Another Beginning?

I was born in April 1942 and have just celebrated another birthday in April 2011. I can look back at the decades of my life to the ten-year-old girl about to be baptised, who showed a public commitment of faith and love for Jesus Christ, her Lord and Saviour. It would take a long time to work out what that step meant but through a very hectic and adventurous life, I began to understand that God who met me on that day has stayed close by and guided every step.

I am almost six decades removed from that little girl and God is the same today as He was yesterday and will be forever. I hold close to me God's words that say:

> Yes, I have taken care of you since you were conceived.
> And have carried you since your birth even to your old age of grey hairs. I am He; I am He who will sustain you.
> I have made you, I will carry you.
> I will sustain you, I will rescue you.

I have reached the stage of grey hairs and experienced the delight of travelling quite long distances on a free bus pass and collecting a weekly pension from the local post office. Yes, approaching advancing years brings other situations with it, and one of the characteristics perhaps is that, as the body becomes more tired or unwell, the spirit inside gets stronger. Luke tells us of two such people in his Gospel. There was Simeon, described as a good and devout man who was able to see the child Jesus, God's promised Messiah. Then there was the prophetess Anna, who was eighty-four years old and by the same devotion was able to see the truth about Jesus.

I suppose there is also the added advantage that we don't rush about quite as much as we did when in secular professions, ministry or with busy families and growing children. But wherever we are, we can be sure that God is with us.

My early life overseas and my life at home has been a mirror image, a reflection thrusting me out into the hurly-burly of life on to the front line when prayers become more of a part of our lives than the luxury of quiet space to experience the presence and reality of God.

I often think now, when life is still very busy, how comforted I am by the words spoken by the Cistercian monks, "to work is to pray". St Teresa also found God amongst domestic tasks and Brother Lawrence could turn a loving gaze to God when elbow deep in potato peelings.

Whatever age we are, and whatever circumstances we find ourselves in, we can pray prayers which become as natural as breathing. Prayers for help, strength, courage, thanksgiving, adoration, while standing in a queue, stuck in a traffic jam, drinking a cup of coffee, washing the dishes, all bringing to us the constant awareness and presence of God.

Sometimes during very difficult times I have been asked, "Didn't that cause you to lose your faith? You have been in church all your life. Didn't you ever feel you wanted to leave it?" As Christians we are expected to grow, to mature – stickability and tenacity helping us to hold on when things don't turn out quite the way we expect them to. Through it all we are greatly loved by God and encouraged to persevere. As one gets older, it can be tempting to plateau off and be content with yesterday's experiences of God. But God wants to go on meeting us in all areas of our lives, often pressing on through our seventieth, eightieth and ninetieth years.

As I reflected on those words I thought, well, I still have some space left and with God's grace there may still be more to come. Perhaps there will still be more adventures, more stories and one thing I am really sure of is that there will be lots of Him. I smiled to myself when I read these words in a local newspaper: 'The aim of enjoying life is not to edge towards the grave slowly to be placed silently inside, rather to hurtle towards it and skid in sideways yelling: "Wow, that was a heck of a ride!"'

Life can be great fun with all its surprising twists and turns and life with God can certainly be fun with the added promise that life doesn't end in the grave but continues into eternity with Him.

These moments shared with you have been precious to me. I hope you have enjoyed them as I have enjoyed living through them. In light and darkness, tears and laughter, joy and pain, life is still fulfilling and challenging.

Circumstances change. For the first time in my life I find myself attending hospital and waiting for results and decisions. As I ponder and chat to God about it all, I am reminded of words from *Sadhana: A Way to God* by Anthony DeMello: 'Don't push the river... It flows by itself and so does life. Don't push. "Happiness" is letting the happenings happen.'

And finally a great favourite of mine from the same book is the vision of Dame Julian of Norwich, 'Christ laughed out loud and told her: "All things shall be well, and all manner of things shall be well."'

Wherever you are, and whatever your circumstances are, can I leave you with just those few words?

All things shall be well.

Margaret

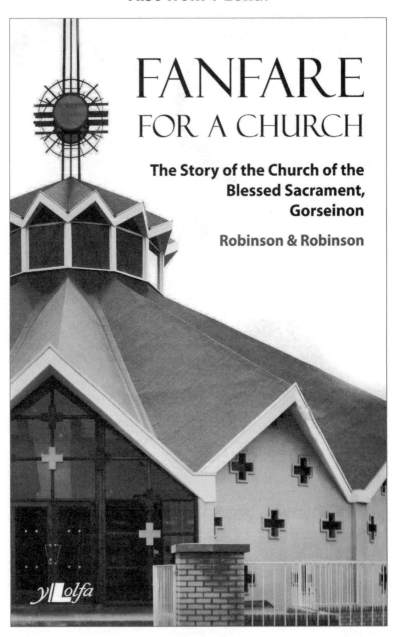

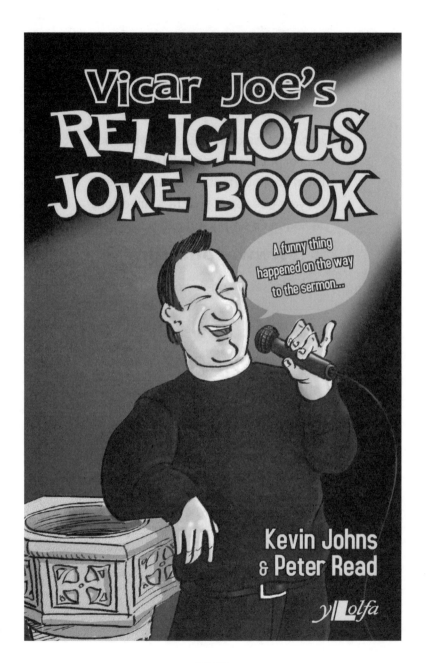

£4.95

Decades of Discovery is just one of a whole range of publications from Y Lolfa. For a full list of books currently in print, send now for your free copy of our new full-colour catalogue. Or simply surf into our website

www.ylolfa.com

for secure on-line ordering.

TALYBONT CEREDIGION CYMRU SY24 5HE
e-mail ylolfa@ylolfa.com
website www.ylolfa.com
phone (01970) 832 304
fax 832 782